Supervision in the helping professions

Supervision in the helping professions

An individual, group and organizational approach

PETER HAWKINS and
ROBIN SHOHET

OPEN UNIVERSITY PRESS
Milton Keynes • Philadelphia

Open University Press
Celtic Court
22 Ballmoor
Buckingham MK18 1XW

and
1900 Frost Road, Suite 101
Bristol, PA 19007, USA

First published 1989
Reprinted 1990 (twice), 1991, 1992, 1993

British Library Cataloguing in Publication Data

Hawkins, Peter
    Supervision in the helping professions: an individual, group
    and organizational approach.
    1. Great Britain. Social services. Personnel management.
    I. Title   II. Shohet, Robin
    361'.068'3

    ISBN 0–335–09854–1
    ISBN 0–335–09833–9 (pbk)

Library of Congress Cataloging-in-Publication Data

Hawkins, Peter
    Supervision in the helping professions: an individual, group, and
    organizational approach / Peter Hawkins and Robin Shohet.
        p. cm.
    Bibliography: p.
    Includes index.
    ISBN 0–335–09854–1   ISBN 0–335–09833–9 (pbk.)
    1. Counselors—Supervision of.   2. Social workers—Supervision of.
I. Shohet, Robin.   II. Title.
BF637.C6H365   1989
361.3'23'0683—dc20   89–9261
                                                              CIP

Typeset by Burns & Smith, Derby
Printed and bound in Great Britain by
Biddles Ltd, Guildford and King's Lynn

To all our supervisors and supervisees,
especially those who were with us in our formative years
at St Charles House of the Richmond Fellowship

'quis custodiet ipsos custodes?'
(who will care and protect the carers?)

Juvenal VI: *347–8.*

Contents

Acknowledgements

We would like first to thank Brian Wade of Changes bookshop for the initial idea of writing this book.

Much of the material on which this book is based has been developed over the last twelve years in the training courses in supervision we have been running through the Centre for Staff Team Development. Joan Wilmot made a substantial contribution to both the creation and teaching of these courses and has been a source of inspiration to us both.

Many colleagues have been very generous with their own ideas and experience of supervision, especially Frank Kevlin, Alix Pirani, Brigid Proctor, Helen Davis, Terry Cooper and Hymie Wyse. Mary Parker and Michael Carroll helped us find our way around the American literature on supervision. Adrian McLean and Marsha George of Bath Associates both made important contributions to the section of the book on organizations.

Monica Brooks relieved the last-minute panics in typing the bibliography and photocopying the manuscript.

Annie Spencer and Ingrid Johansson both gave us timely supervision on our co-writing.

Several people generously provided a quiet refuge in which to write. In this respect we would especially like to thank Tony and Jean Wheilden of Grimstone Manor, Peter Tatham and Gregynog Hall of the University of Wales.

Finally we would like to thank our partners Judy Ryde and Joan Wilmot and all our children for their patience and their support in the anti-social activity of writing the book.

PART ONE

The supervisee's perspective

1 'Good-enough' supervision

The late Donald Winnicott, paediatrician and psychoanalyst, introduced the concept of the 'good-enough mother' – the mother who, when her child throws the food back at her, does not over-react to this event as a personal attack, or sink under feelings of inadequacy and guilt, but can hear this event as the child's expressing its temporary inability to cope with the external world. Winnicott points out that it is very hard for any mother to be 'good-enough' unless she herself is also held and supported, either by the child's father, or other supportive adult. This provides the 'nursing triad', which means that the child can be held even when it needs to express his or her negativity or murderous rage.

This concept provides a very useful analogy for supervision, where the 'good-enough' counsellor, psychotherapist or other helping professional can survive the negative attacks of the client through the strength of being held within and by the supervisory relationship. We have often seen very competent workers reduced to severe doubts about themselves and their abilities to function in the work through absorbing disturbance from clients. The supervisor's role is not just to reassure the worker, but to allow the emotional disturbance to be felt within the safer setting of the supervisory relationship, where it can be survived, reflected upon and learnt from. Supervision thus provides a container that holds the helping relationship within the 'therapeutic triad'.

In choosing to help, where our role is to pay attention to someone else's needs, we are entering into a relationship which is different from the normal and everyday. There are times when it seems barely worthwhile, perhaps because we are battling against the odds, or because the client is ungrateful, or because we feel drained and have seemingly nothing left to give. In times of stress it is sometimes easy to keep one's head down, to 'get on with it' and not take time to reflect. Organizations, teams and individuals can collude with this attitude for a variety of reasons, including external pressures and internal fears of exposing one's own inadequacies.

At times like this supervision can be very important. It can give us a chance to stand back and reflect; a chance to avoid the easy ways out of blaming others – clients, peers, the organization, 'society', or even oneself; and it can give us a chance to engage in the search for new options, to discover the learning that often emerges from the most difficult situations, and to get support. We believe that, if the value and experience of good supervision are realized at the beginning of one's professional career, then the 'habit' of receiving good supervision will become an integral part of the work life and the continuing development of the worker.

In the last five years there has been an enormous increase in the use of counselling and therapeutic approaches in many of the helping professions. This has in part been fuelled by the move away from more traditional forms of institutional containment to 'community care' for those needing help and support. This move has led to an ever increasing demand, not just on families and relatives, but also on the whole range of helping professionals who have had to learn new ways of relating to the distress, disturbance and fragmentation of their clients. At the same time there has been an increased acceptance by the general public that most people need some form of counselling at certain stages of their lives.

This enormous upsurge in both counselling and psychotherapy, and in counselling and therapeutic approaches within many of the helping professions, has brought in its wake the recognition that such work needs to be properly supervised. The need for skilled supervisors, good training in supervision, and for theory and research in this area has increased much faster than the provision. In Britain there are very few books on supervision, and those that do exist are mainly limited to one profession. There is also a dearth of theoretical papers and descriptive accounts by those practising supervision. Only in the last two years has the British Association of Counselling started to look at the training and accreditation of supervisors and have psychotherapy training institutes started to provide training courses in this crucial area of work.

In the United States they have been concerned with this core area of practice much longer. In the last ten years there has been a great number of American papers and books on supervision. However, much of the work has been within the discipline of 'counselling psychology' and has mostly centred around one particular model – namely 'the developmental approach'. Although this is a significant contribution (see Chapter 5), it attends to only one of the many important aspects of the supervisory process.

The supervisor has to integrate the role of educator with that of being the provider of support to the worker and, in most cases, managerial oversight of the supervisee's clients. These three functions do not always sit comfortably together (see Chapter 5), and many supervisors can retreat from attempting this integration to just one of the roles. Some supervisors become quasi-counsellors to their supervisees; others turn supervision into a two-person case-conference, which focuses on client dynamics; others may have a managerial check-list with which they 'check-up' on the client management of the supervisee. It is our intention in this book to help the supervisor develop an integrated style of supervision. We are not only advocating integration of the educative, supportive and managerial roles, but also a supervisory approach which is relationship based.

Sometimes, even in the best supervisory relationships, there will be times of being stuck, of wariness and even of avoidance. For one reason or another fear and negativity can creep in and it is useful for both parties to be able to recognize this and have tools for going through and beyond it. This book is addressed to both supervisor and supervisee, for we think that both have some responsibility for the quality of supervision; both form part of the same system geared towards ensuring quality of work. As part of taking joint responsibility for the supervisory relationship which we are advocating, we have therefore given guidelines to check out the process, especially around the initial forming of a contract for the working relationship. This working contract can be very important as it forms the boundaries and baseline to which both parties can refer.

Before entering this relationship, however, we believe that supervision begins with self-supervision; and this begins with appraising one's motives and facing parts of ourselves we would normally keep hidden (even from our own awareness) as honestly as possible. By doing this we can lessen the split that sometimes occurs in the helpers, whereby they believe they are problem free and have no needs, and see their clients as only sick and needy. As Margaret Rioch (1976) says: 'If students do not know that they are potentially murderers, crooks and cowards, they cannot deal therapeutically with these potentialities in their clients.'

Our experience has been that supervision can be a very important part of taking care of oneself, staying open to new learning, and an indispensable part of the helper's ongoing self-development, self-awareness and commitment to learning. In some professions, however, supervision is virtually ignored after qualifying. We think that lack of supervision can contribute to feelings of staleness, rigidity and defensiveness which can very easily occur in professions that require us to give so much of ourselves. In extremes the staleness and defensiveness contribute to the syndrome which recent writers have termed 'burnout'. Supervision can help to stop this process by breaking the cycle of feeling drained which leads to a drop in work standards which produces guilt and inadequacy which lead to a further drop in standards.

Supervision, like helping, is not a straightforward process and is even more complex than working with clients. There is no tangible product and very little evidence whereby we can rigorously assess its effectiveness. One person brings to another a client, usually never seen by the supervisor, and reports very selectively on aspects of the work. Moreover, there may be all sorts of pressures on either or both of them from the profession, organization or society in which they both work. So, as well as dealing with the client in question, they have to pay attention to their supervisory relationship and the wider systems in which they both operate. There is a danger that both the supervisee and the supervisor can be overwhelmed by the degree of complexity and become like the centipede who, when asked which foot it moved first, lost the ability to move.

In order to encompass the complex interconnecting levels of the supervision process and yet write a book that is comprehensible, we have divided the book into four parts.

In the first part we have addressed the supervisees with the intention of encouraging them to be proactive in managing to get the support they need to do their work. Helping organizations and managers have an important responsibility to attend to the well-being of their staff, but it is only the workers themselves who can ensure that they get the particular type of support that is most appropriate for them and their work situation. There is a danger for workers to see support as coming only from higher up in their organization and to fail to see that support for their work can arrive from many different directions. Even within the supervisory relationship it is important that the supervisees can find a way of being active in ensuring that they make the most of the relationship. In this section we have also included a chapter on the motives for being a helper which is relevant for supervisor and supervisee alike.

In the second section we look at making the transition from working with clients to becoming a supervisor, the different roles and functions that are involved, and the maps and models which we have found useful. Some of the same ground as Chapter 3 will be covered, but from the point of view of the supervisor. Chapter 6 is an in-depth exploration of the various aspects and levels of the supervisory relationship. This chapter is particularly addressed to those supervisors who supervise counsellors, psychotherapists or other professionals who are working in intensive therapeutic relationships (such as psychiatrists, psychologists, nurse therapists, etc.). The section ends with a chapter which explores the training needed for different types of supervisors – for those who supervise front-line staff; those who supervise students or trainees; those who supervise teams and those who supervise departments or whole organizations. This chapter is both for those supervisors who want to think about what training they need for themselves and also for trainers, training officers and others who are responsible for providing training in supervision.

In the third section we look at forms of supervision other than the one to one, such as supervision in groups, peer groups and in work teams. This section explores the advantages and disadvantages of supervising individuals in a group setting and some of the ways of managing the group dynamics. It also explores how to supervise teams in a way that recognizes that the team is more than the sum of the individuals contained within it.

In the final section we focus on how to help an organization develop a learning culture where supervision is an intrinsic part of the work environment. We have found that the organizational context in which supervision occurs has a major influence on the supervisory relationship.

Focusing on this wider context helps in the understanding of the wider system in which supervision occurs. This understanding can be useful in not over-personalizing a problem which is also a symptom of the organizational dynamics and in realizing that it is not just individual workers nor indeed just work teams that need supervision, but whole helping organizations. In Chapter 10 we also look at the need for supervising situations where a number of professional helpers and organizations are involved and the specialized skills that this requires.

We end with a concluding chapter that pulls together the various themes of the book and returns us once more to the theme of the next chapter, ourselves as wounded helpers.

We saw the four parts as increasing in complexity, starting with one person, the helper, then a supervisory relationship, then groups, then organizations. However we recognize that looking at the internal processes of ourselves can be as complex as looking at the organizational dynamics – it just involves fewer people. This choice of topic and order has been meaningful for us, but our hope is that the actual topics become less important in themselves and become triggers for your own experience and action.

Another notion that we take from Winnicott is that learning is most creative when it emerges in play. In the supervision that we give we try and create a climate which avoids the sense of expert and student both studying the client 'out there' and instead creates a 'play space' in which the dynamics and pressures of the work can be felt, explored and understood; and where new ways of working can be co-created by both supervisor and supervisee working together. Likewise in this book we have shared our experience of the feelings, issues and possibilities of supervision in order to create more choices and options for both supervisee and supervisor.

We also recommend that you choose your own order for reading the chapters, for as we have indicated above, each section (and indeed each chapter) is addressed to a slightly different audience. However, we suggest that all readers start with Chapters 2 and 3, as, no matter how experienced you are as a supervisor, or even as a trainer of supervisors, we all share in common the need constantly to look at why we are in the work and how we get appropriate support for ourselves.

2 Why be a helper?

Without minimizing the external demands of helping others, it seems fair to say that some of the factors that wear us down, we have brought with us at the outset.

(Ram Dass and Paul Gorman 1985)

No one can act out of exclusively pure motives. The greater the contamination by dark motives, the more the case worker clings to his alleged objectivity.

(Guggenbühl-Craig 1971)

With great puzzlement and a furrowed brow he said, 'I don't understand why you are so angry with me. I wasn't trying to help you'.

(attributed to Wilfred Bion and quoted by Symington 1986)

How can I help is a timeless enquiry of the heart.

(Ram Dass and Paul Gorman 1985)

In this chapter we will look at some of the complex motives for wanting to work in the helping or caring professions. As the quotations above indicate, we do not think these motives are clear and simple. Sometimes helper and helpee are caught in a tangle of mutual misunderstanding, both feeling powerless but unable to share this. The role of helper carries with it certain expectations. Sometimes clinging to our roles makes it difficult to see the strengths in our clients, the vulnerability in ourselves as helpers, and our interdependence. As Ram Dass says (1985): 'The more you think of yourself as a "therapist", the more pressure there is for someone to be "patient".' In choosing to start here, we are again saying that a willingness to examine our motives, 'good' or 'bad', pure or otherwise, is a prerequisite for being an effective helper. Aware of what Jungians call our 'shadow' side, we will have less need to make others into the parts of ourselves we cannot accept. The crazy psychiatric patient will not have to carry our own craziness, while we pretend to be completely sane; in the cancer patients who cannot face their impending death, we will see our own fear of dying. Focusing on our shadow, we will be less prone to omnipotent fantasies of changing others or the world, when we cannot change ourselves.

One aspect of his own shadow – the wish for praise/adulation – happened to Robin while we were writing this book.

I was running a residential therapy group abroad on my own. After a group member had worked on her feelings involving the death of a child, the group began to share at a very deep level, with one person's work triggering off another's. As the group facilitator I found the work both rewarding and moving as people resolved some of their deep pain. Staying with the process was for me tiring, yet paradoxically effortless in the way people's openness allowed their work to unfold. I could not remember any group which had consistently managed to face such trauma, and work through it successfully. At times like this I remember how privileged I am to be a witness to such work. At times like this ego creeps in. Look what *I* have done as facilitator. After the fourth session we sat around for dinner. I missed not having a co-leader and was wanting the group to give me some validation for (my) wonderful work. Just then a wasp came and joined us. I ran. There was much laughter. 'So you are human after all.' I laughed too, but not before I had caught a feeling of resentment at being lovingly mocked and not revered.

How often we find ourselves caught in the shadow side of helping, letting ourself and others think we are special, creating that illusion, and then being disillusioned when people want to take us down a peg or two.

The idea that we are helpers as opposed to a channel for help is a dangerous one. We want the praise for the success, but not the blame for the failure. Both of us struggle with the idea of non-attachment, telling students and clients who thank us for good pieces of work that it is not us, but themselves they should thank, yet secretly saying '... and me'. It is hard really to accept the possibility of being only the vehicle of help. Yet this acceptance is the only way to get off the roundabout of being addicted to praise and fearful of blame, and to stop ourselves lurching wildly between impotence and omnipotence.

Non-attachment does not mean not caring. On the contrary it may be the nearest we can get to real caring as we do not have to live through our clients, dependent on their successes for our self-esteem.

In different ways we were given the opportunity to learn this lesson early on in our helping careers working in a residential therapeutic community. The supervisor of the home came fortnightly to supervise the head of the establishment and then to do a group supervision for all the staff. In one of these sessions the staff were engaged in an intense exchange around how to treat one of the residents. The supervisor stopped the discussion in its tracks by saying:

You are not here to treat the residents, nor are you here to heal them or make them better. The job of the staff is to maintain the structure and keep open the space in which the residents can learn and grow. You are merely the servants of the process.

We had to learn (and are still learning) to give up the struggle for omnipotence, to let go of the idea that we were the ones that cured people, and learn the humility of being the care taker of the therapeutic space.

Yet humility too is not without danger. The word 'caretaker' reminds us of a Jewish joke.

One day a rabbi has an ecstatic vision and rushes up before the ark in his synagogue and prostrates himself, saying: 'Lord, Lord, in Thine eyes I am nothing.' The cantor (singer) of the synagogue, not wishing to be outdone, also rushes up to the altar and prostrates himself saying: 'Lord, Lord, in Thine eyes I am nothing.' The shamash (caretaker) sees the other two and decides to do the same. He rushes up and prostrates himself with the same words: 'Lord, Lord, in Thine eyes I am nothing.' Whereupon the rabbi turns to the cantor and says: 'Look who thinks he's nothing.'

A book that deals very succinctly and challengingly with the shadow side of helping is *Power in the Helping Professions* by Guggenbühl-Craig (1971). He writes (p. 79):

To expand our understanding ... perhaps it is necessary to go more deeply into what it is that drives the members of these ministering professions to do the kind of work they do. What prompts the psychotherapist to try to help people in emotional difficulty? What urges the psychiatrist to deal with the mentally ill? Why does the social worker concern himself with social misfits?

Here is Peter's story in response to that question.

I originally believed that I would work in the creative arts and that I was destined for a career in the theatre or television, but I was drawn away from performance to working in community arts, dramatherapy and from there into mental health work. I worked with people who were actively psychotic, who had murdered, burnt down churches, were violent, suicidal, alcoholic etc. – the whole gamut of human anguish, distress and pain. In this work I found relief, which many of my friends found strange, but which I now know was the relief that my own buried disturbance, hidden and denied within my family, school and culture within which I grew up, now had an outward reality. It was all being played out in the therapeutic community in which I worked.

Looking back I can recognize that I both did some very good work which came from a genuine wanting (and needing) to meet these people in their pain, but also I had, eventually, to move on from this work as I had not got to the stage where I could re-own the full depths of my own shadow disturbance that these clients were living out for me. I had not truly faced my own inner murderer, my paranoid fear, my fragmentation, my despair. So I was unable to meet them fully as equals and was only able to come alongside in an unequal relationship where they carried the dis-ease and I was reinforced in my role of the coping, caring and containing worker.

The journey from facing my own dark inner self through others, back home to facing the shadow deep within myself has been and is a long and painful process. It isn't one simple cycle, but many small waves of discovering depths within others that I then need to go back and find in myself. Now that I work as a psychotherapist I have a simple rule that if I find myself saying something more than twice to different clients, trainees or supervisees, I assume that I am also saying this to myself and I go away, write it down and explore it.

For most of us the answer to the question of 'why', would include the wish to care, to cure, to heal – an attraction to the 'healer-patient archetype'. Alongside this, however, may be a hidden need for power, both in surrounding oneself with people worse off, and being able to direct parts of the lives of the people who need help. Guggenbühl-Craig (1975) also addresses this issue:

> In my years of analytical work with social workers, I have noticed time and time again that whenever something must be imposed by force, the conscious and unconscious motives of those involved are many faceted. An uncanny lust for power lurks in the background ... Quite frequently, the issue at stake appears to be not the welfare of the protected, but the power of the protector.

This is especially difficult to recognize, because at times of having to make decisions about clients, or their children, the worker very often feels incredibly powerless. This contrasts markedly with the power that he or she has and is seen to have. Here is an example which demonstrates the discrepancy in feelings of power, the value of supervision, and the relevance of understanding motives even when it initially appears irrelevant to do so.

> A client with a record of considerable violence threatened to kill his experienced social worker for removing his child from home. The social worker was understandably anxious at this, the anxiety escalated and could not be held within a loose framework of supervision. I was consulted and felt inadequate to contain this life-threatening anxiety. I decided that the only way I could help was to concentrate on a thorough understanding of the dynamics of the case, although this hardly seemed to be the crisis response that was being asked for. With this focus, we began to understand the covert rivalry between the worker and the parent to be the better parent, and the murderous, unmanageable rage the client experienced when his inferiority was confirmed and concretized by the making of a Care Order. An appreciation of the rivalry served to contain the anxiety in the worker, the agency and myself by providing pointers to planning the work. This served to release the anxious paralysis. The client, I am

thankful to say, responded sufficiently for the situation to become diffused. I quote this example to illustrate my point that agencies concerned with public safety, and indeed the safety of their workers ... let supervision go at their peril.

(Dearnley 1985)

We have come to believe that this case is not as exceptional as it may first look. In our experience, once workers have made a shift in acknowledging some aspect of their shadow side – in this case the competition – there is very often a shift in the client right from the start of the very next meeting.

The issue round the potential misuse of power was put very simply by one worker: 'We dabble in people's lives and make enormous assumptions about what we do. We don't sit back and think about what it really means. We can create dependency, undermine the client's worth ...' (quoted in Fineman 1985). This can be done on a very subtle level. Here is an example from one of our supervisees. It comes from weekly psychotherapy where a male therapist had been seeing a female client in her mid-thirties for about eighteen months.

The client's presenting problem at the therapy session was her difficulties at work. There was a staff member there who was very offhand with her, treating her almost like some kind of servant, and she could not confront him with his obnoxious behaviour, although she very much wanted to. It transpired that this allowing him to treat her like an object even extended to his going to bed with her whenever he wanted. She did not know how to say no, and at some level they both knew this, which is why he could treat her with such contempt.

During the session the therapist suggested that she made an agreement with him, if she wanted, not to sleep with this man for three months, and see if it made any difference to her relationship with him. The following week she came back and said she had felt a lot stronger in the way she interacted with this man, and was very glad about the agreement. The therapist was pleased, but something did not feel right. He took the case to his fortnightly supervision, and realized that he had become just another man telling her what to do – perhaps with more benign intentions, but nevertheless undermining her. The fact that she had agreed to the suggestion and was happy with the outcome almost completely missed the point – namely her underlying problem in all relationships with men, which obviously included the therapist, was that she could not say no. The therapist knew that his suggestion was not a permanent solution, but had not realized how much he and his helpful suggestion was also part of the client's process of giving power to men.

In supervision the therapist faced the fact that it was the 'victim' part of himself which he felt so uneasy about, that had prompted his rush into this premature intervention. He came to realise that rushing into premature solutions was his way of attempting to deal with his own fear of powerlessness. In doing what he had done, he was creating an unnecessary dependence on himself for a behavioural solution instead of doing his job which was to help explore a fuller understanding of how she repeatedly got herself into such situations.

Another aspect of shadow we would like to look at is the helper's attitude to needs – their own needs, both of the job and of their clients. As part of our training we are taught to pay attention to client needs, and it is often difficult to focus on our own needs. It is even considered selfish, self indulgent. Yet our needs are there nonetheless. They are there, we believe, *in our very motives for the work we do.* As James Hillman (1979) writes:

Analysts, counsellors, social workers are all trouble shooters. We are looking for trouble, even before the person comes in to take the waiting chair: 'What's wrong?' 'What's the matter?' The meeting begins not only with the projections of the person coming for help, but the trained and organized intention of the professional helper. In analysis we would say that the countertransference is there before the transference begins. My expectations are there with me as I wait for the knock on the door.

In fact countertransference is there from the beginning, since some unconscious call in me impels me to do this work. I may bring to my work a need to redeem the wounded child, so that every person who comes to me for help is my own hurt wounded childhood needing its wounds bound up by good parental care. Or the reverse: I may still be the wonderful son who would lead his father or mother out of their mistaken ways. This same parent–child archetype may also affect us, for instance, in the need to correct and punish an entire generation, its ideals and values.

My needs are never absent. I could not do this work did I not need to do this work ... Just as the person who comes to me needs me for help, I need him to express my ability to give help. The helper and the needy, the social worker and the social case, the lost and the found, always go together. However we have been brought up to deny our needs. The ideal man of western protestantism shows his 'strong ego' in independence ... Needs in themselves are not harmful, but when they are denied they join the shadows of counselling and work from behind as demands ... Demands ask for fulfilment, needs require only expression.

It is not the needs themselves, but the denial of them that we believe can be so costly. In the next chapter we will look more at the denial of needs, particularly in relation to support. Another need we would like to mention here, however, is the need to be liked, valued, to be seen as doing one's best, to have good intentions even if we sometimes have to make difficult decisions for the 'client's own good': in short, to be seen as the good guy. It is not easy for us, even after many years of working with people and attempting to face our shadow side, to accept a picture of ourselves, painted by a client, which does not correspond with how we see ourselves. It seems so unfair to be told that one is cold, rigid or misusing power. The temptations are either to alter one's behaviour to be more 'pleasing', to counterattack subtly or otherwise, or stop working with the person for 'plausible' reasons. The ingratitude is sometimes hard to accept. We may find ourselves thinking, '... after all I've done for you', words we heard from a parent or teacher, and which we promised never to repeat.

One of the best ways we have found of accepting some of these negative feelings from clients (which usually have at least a grain of truth in them) is for us to remember how *we* feel as clients. We can also remember how in our own supervision, when we feel inadequate, we want to criticize our supervisors in order to make them feel as we do.

It would seem from the above that it is almost worth packing it in. The chapter has been full of lurking power drives, needy children, unclear motives, hostility to parents. To think this would be to miss the point alluded to above – namely it is only the *denial* of needs, shadow, image, power that makes them dangerous. Knowing ourselves, our motives and our needs, makes us more likely to be of real help. In that way we do not use others unawarely for our own ends, or make them carry bits of ourselves we cannot face. For we believe that the desire to help, in spite of the unclarity surrounding it, *is* fundamental, and agree with Harold Searles (1975) when he says that:

> innate among man's most powerful strivings towards his fellow men, beginning in the earliest years and even earliest months, is an essentially psychotherapeutic striving. The tiny percentage of human beings who devote their professional careers to the practice of psychoanalysis or psychotherapy are only giving explicit expression to a therapeutic devotion which all human beings share ... I am hypothesizing that the patient is ill because, and to the degree that his own psychotherapeutic strivings have been subjected to such vicissitudes that they have been rendered inordinately intense, frustrated of fulfilment or even acknowledgement, admixed therefore with unduly intense components of hate, envy and competitiveness: and subjected therefore to repression. In transference terms the patient's illness expresses his unconscious attempt to cure the doctor.

In other words the wish to heal is basic to helpers and non-helpers alike.

We have found that when we have been able to accept our own vulnerability and not defend against it, it has been a valuable experience both for us and our clients. The realization that they could be healing us, as much as the other way round, has been very important both in their relationship with us and their growth. It is another reminder that we are servants of the process.

Finally, we believe that we are only in a position to give when our own needs go some way to being acknowledged and satisfied. To give when we feel that we have something to give, and not just when the client demands, or when we feel we 'ought' to. This puts a lot of responsibility on helpers to be active in trying to satisfy their own needs. It is this we will turn to in the next chapter.

3 Getting the support and supervision you need

A social worker spoke with poignancy about her difficulties in coping with the demands of a particular client when added to her home pressures. I asked her if she had shared her concerns with her colleagues. 'Oh no!' she retorted, 'I wouldn't want to be social worked by them.' She then recoiled with a look of horror on her face, 'God, what am I saying? I can use my social work skills on clients but I can't accept them for myself?'

(in Fineman 1985)

Many helpers, when they themselves are suffering are incapable of accepting support, or at least receiving it easily. Yet they may be impatient with those they're working with for not accepting aid or counsel readily enough. Chances are, if you can't accept help, you can't really give it.

(Ram Dass 1985)

'I cannot get the support and supervision I need to do my job as my manager is either too busy or too inadequate to give me good supervision.' This is regularly said to us by workers in a great variety of helping professions. Teachers, probation officers, social workers and doctors will often complain that they are constantly drained by supporting so many clients and patients, but receive very little support themselves.

In the previous chapter we explored how this in part may be due to the addiction to giving, which is a defence against being a person who needs support oneself. In this chapter we will look at how, even when you acknowledge the need for support, it is still possible to remain stuck blaming others for not providing it. We will explore ways of moving out of this passive position into taking responsibility for ensuring that you get the support and supervision you need. This is a fundamental shift from being re-active and dependent to being pro-active concerning your own support system.

It is in the spirit of being pro-active that we would like you to read this chapter. As you read through it, we would like to give you the opportunity to take stock of your own support system, your stress and how you manage it. We would also like you to evaluate your own supervision and explore how it can better meet your needs. This chapter is also for supervisors, for to be a good supervisor is also to be a pro-active supervisee, ensuring that you continue to arrange and use support for yourself, and can model this to your staff. We also hope that the chapter will provide ways in which supervisors can encourage autonomy and pro-activity in their supervisees.

Mapping your support system

We would like you to start by taking a large sheet of paper (A3 or bigger) and on it draw a map of your support system at work. In the middle of the paper draw a symbol or picture of yourself. Then around this picture or symbol draw pictures, symbols, diagrams or words to represent all the things and people that support you in learning and being creative at work. These may be the walk to work, books you read, colleagues, meetings, friends, etc. We would like you to represent the nature of your connection to these supports. Are they near or far away? Is the link strong and regular or tenuous or distant? Are they supporting you from below like foundations or are they balloons that lift you up? These are only suggestions; allow yourself to find your own way of mapping your support system.

When you are satisfied with your initial map, we would like you to take a completely different colour and draw on the picture symbols that represent those things that block you from fully using these supports. It may be fear of being criticized or interruptions or the relative unavailability of these supports. It may be blocks within you, within the support, or in the organizational setting. Draw whatever you feel stops you getting the support you need.

When you have done this, we would suggest that you choose someone with whom to share your picture. This could be a colleague, partner, supervisor or friend, or even someone who has also done the exercise (you could get your whole staff team to do it!). When you have shared your picture with them, they should first respond to the overall picture. What impression does it create? Then they can ask you the following questions:

- Is this the kind of support you want?
- Is it enough? What sort of support is missing? How could you go about getting such support?
- What support is really positive for you to the extent that you must ensure that you nurture and maintain it?
- Which blocks could you do something about reducing?

Your partner could then encourage you to develop some specific action plans as to how you might improve your support system. The action plan should include, *what* you are going to do; *how* you are going to do it; *when* and *where* you are going to do it; and involving *whom*?

If there is no one that you want to share this process with, it is possible to do the exercise by yourself and ask yourself these questions, but it is much more difficult. Also, involving another is a good first step in pro-actively asking for support!

Stress

What happens if you do not have enough support is that you absorb more disturbance, distress and dis-ease from your clients and patients than you are able to process and let go of and then you become overburdened by the work. Stress is not only absorbed from the clients but may also come from other aspects of the work and the organization in which you work. These stressors (factors causing stress) will in turn interact with your own personality and the stressors that are currently happening in your own life outside work.

Fineman (1985) provides a useful and simple model illustrating the inter-connectedness of stress and support (Figure 3.1). The diagram underlines the importance of not only attending to, and taking responsibility for, your own support system, but also ensuring that you are taking responsibility for responding actively to the stressors in your own work and home life.

Figure 3.1   Facets of social worker stress

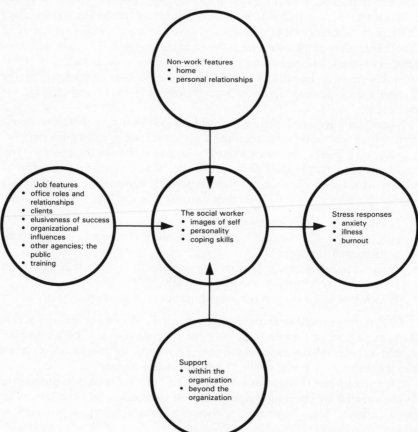

Some stress is inevitable and can be positive in activating the body, mind and energies of the worker. It can awaken our energies ready for action and for dealing with a threat or a crisis. However, so often in the helping professions the stressors of the work charge our mental and bodily systems ready for action, but there is no possibility for discharging this energy into action. We are left having to sit with the pain of the patient; or having to contain the frustration of not being able to secure the funding to meet client needs that we are in touch with; or having to cope with situations in which we feel undertrained or emotionally inadequate.

Stress that is not discharged stays within the body and can emerge as physical, mental or emotional symptoms. It is important to know your own tendencies for responding to stress, so you can be alert to the build-up of tension within you. In Table 3.1 we offer examples of some of the most common symptoms of being stressed, but suggest that you stop and make a note of the symptoms that inform you that you are overstressed. You might also take the opportunity to ask those who work with you, how they notice that you are under pressure?

Table 3.1 Symptoms of stress

Physical
1 Migraines or headaches.
2 Diarrhoea, indigestion, constipation.
3 Insomnia.
4 Overtiredness.
5 Loss of appetite.

Mental
1 Inability to concentrate.
2 Compulsive worry.
3 Paranoid thoughts, seeing yourself as victim.

Behavioural
1 Pretending to care, and playing the role of carer, but the actions and feelings are incongruous.
2 Avoiding clients, colleagues or situations.
3 Turning to drink, over-eating or over-smoking.

Emotional
1 Sudden swings in feelings.
2 Not wanting to get up in the mornings.
3 'Floating anxiety'.
4 Hating clients.

It is very important that, as helpers, we take responsibility for noticing the signs that our systems are overloaded: and that we ensure that we get the support, not only to deal with the symptoms of stress that are emerging within us, but also to tackle the cause of the stress. The earlier this is done the better. If we ignore the stress symptoms for too long then we are in danger of being overwhelmed and being left in a situation where the only things we can attend to are the resultant symptoms within us. When this happens we have entered the state that is often referred to as 'burnout'.

Burnout

The term 'burnout' has, in recent years, become much overused. It has become the helping professions' equivalent to what the British army called 'shell shock' or the Americans 'battle fatigue'; what our parents' generation called 'nerves' and the present generation 'depression'. They become catch-all phrases that signify not coping. Burnout is not an illness that you catch, neither is it a recognizable event or state, for it is a process that often begins very early in one's career as a helper. Indeed its seeds may be inherent in the belief systems of many of the helping professions and in the personalities of those that are attracted to them (see previous chapter).

Edelwich and Brodsky (1980) explore how unrealistically high expectations of what can be achieved can create the background for the later development of disillusionment and apathy. Many professions also encourage their trainees to develop the image of themselves as heroic helpers who can continually provide for others, solving their problems, feeling their pain, meeting their needs, whilst remaining themselves strong and happy. This can be coupled with the personality of those attracted to such work who may have been the one who contained the pain and was always helpful in their own families.

Pines *et al.* (1981) define burnout as:

the result of constant or repeated *emotional pressure* associated with an intense involvement with people over long periods of time. Such intense involvement is particularly prevalent in health, education and social service occupations, where professionals have a 'calling' to take care of other people's psychological, social and physical problems. Burnout is the painful realization that they no longer can help people in need, that they have nothing left in them to give.

Fineman (1985) follows Maslach (1982) in saying that burnout represents:

(a) a state of emotional and physical exhaustion with a lack of concern for the job, and a low trust of others, (b) a depersonalization of clients; a loss of caring and cynicism towards them, and (c) self-deprecation and low morale and a deep sense of failure.

We would contend that the best time to attend to burnout is before it happens. This involves looking at your shadow motivation for being in the helping professions, as explored in the previous chapter; monitoring your own stress symptoms and managing a healthy support system, as explored above; and ensuring that you have a meaningful, enjoyable and physically active life outside the role of being a helper.

In an earlier work (Hawkins 1986) we explored another aspect of burnout that is ignored in most of the literature, which is the apathy and loss of interest which develop in helpers who stop learning and developing in mid-career. They begin to rely on set patterns of relating to clients and patients and treat new clients as just repeat representatives of clients and patients they met earlier in their career. A preventative approach to burnout needs to include creating a learning environment that continues right through one's career as a helper.

Arranging appropriate supervision

There are many reasons to be pro-active in getting good supervision for ourselves. First, supervision is a central form of support, where we can focus on our own difficulties as a worker as well as have our supervisor share some of the responsibility for our work with the clients. Second, supervision forms part of our continual learning and development as workers, including eventually helping us to learn how to be supervisors. A good supervisor can also help us to use our own resources better, manage our workload and challenge our inappropriately patterned ways of coping. We think that, if we are helping clients take more charge of their own lives, it is essential that we are doing the same. Finally, there is research to show that good supervision correlates with job satisfaction (Cherniss and Egnatios 1978).

Blocks to getting supervision

Part of arranging for good supervision is recognizing blocks and finding effective ways of overcoming them. Some of these blocks include: (a) previous experiences of supervision; (b) personal inhibition; (c) difficulties in the supervisory relationship; (d) organizational blocks; (e) practical blocks, such as finance or geography; (f) the culture of the organization or profession's being antithetical to supervision; or a combination of these.

(a) Previous experience of supervision Previous experiences of supervision, both good and bad can influence the current supervision. A bad experience can lead a supervisee to be wary, but a good one can lead to comparisons – no one will be as good as my last supervisor. Taking a more positive stance, you might like to make a résumé of past experiences of supervision and what you learnt from them both in terms of managing the relationship, yourself and skills. How do your needs differ now from then?

(b) Personal inhibition Sometimes just being in a one-to-one relationship can restimulate painful feelings. Here is an account of one supervision relationship from a supervisee on a counselling course:

> When I started supervision I found that I was not going to be directed
> in any way and that all the ideas had to come from me. This felt very

uncomfortable and I felt very much 'on the spot' – in fact it gave an insight as to how a client would feel. Painful emotions were just below the surface brought there by the insecurity of the position I seemed to be in. I felt very vulnerable as if the supervisor's attention was scrutiny. My defensive reaction to this was anger and one week I was on the point of walking out. I actually started to gather my things together. The supervisor stopped me and I realized that I was checking to see if he could cope with my anger. I had a shock of recognition at this scene as it reminded me of how I test out other relationships.

Although these sessions were painful I realized how important supervision was and how necessary for our particular work – especially the 'coping collusion' which permeates our work, our denial of how much we are affected by the client group. Finally the blocks in supervision were self imposed and therefore having another supervisor would not have solved these blocks but brought out others.

The idea of being on the spot, even though objectively there is no assessment, can relate to internal judging. As the above supervisee said:

In all the supervision sessions there was a third person present, a part of myself – very critical – who looked at all my thoughts, actions and feelings and commented on them. Somehow it seemed as if my own analysis of my behaviour served to paralyse me. I always had a counter argument for anything I came up with. It seems as if this is the way I keep control.

We can certainly identify with this, and have often found ourselves being needlessly defensive in supervision, protecting ourselves from being judged, when in fact we are usually the worst judges of ourselves. It can certainly feel very exposing to bring cases to supervision to find out that one has missed something which in retrospect seems very obvious.

You might like to ask yourself here how much you hold back in supervision and for what reasons. Can you share any of these reasons with your supervisor even if it feels a bit risky? Recognizing that supervision can produce anxiety in supervisees, Kadushin (1968) has written about the various strategies adopted by supervisees for dealing with such feelings and we would recommend his paper. There is also a later one by Hawthorne (1975) which looks at supervisor strategies for dealing with *their* anxieties which we will be referring to later.

(c) The supervisory relationship Transference difficulties, usually the projecting of critical or uncontaining parental images are often there, just as in therapy, but less easy to recognize. As one worker said in Fineman's study (1985): 'I fear authority and always feel I need to *prove* to my supervisor that I can do my work.' So supervisors are often not seen for who they are; sometimes they are given too much power, at other times they may be defensively rubbished. Sibling rivalry can also occur in terms of who can

manage the client better, and this can come just as much from the supervisor as the supervisee.

(d) Organizational blocks   There can also be problems around the dual role of supervision of management and support.

> I have regular meetings with my supervisor, but always steer clear of my problems in coping with my report work. Can I trust her? I need her backing for my career progress, but will she use this sort of thing as evidence against me? There are some painful areas that are never discussed but need discussing so much. It's an awful dilemma for me.
>
> (in Fineman 1985)

There was also an appreciation of the dilemma of the supervisor. 'Currently I get supervised by the team leader – but he's in a conflict situation between being a manager and being my supervisor' (in Fineman 1985).

Although supervisors might try to protect their workers from their own stress, the stress was inevitably picked up. Sometimes the supervisees had the attitude 'They've got enough on their plates without my problems', but often there was resentment at not having the support they felt they had a right to.

A mismatch of expectations that never get tackled can play a part in reducing the worth of supervision. 'My supervisor doesn't really provide what I want. He tends to pick on things which are important to him, not me' (in Fineman 1985).

We will explore later in this chapter the importance of ensuring that you have a clear supervision contract with your supervisor, and that roles and expectations within the supervision are explored and regularly reviewed.

(e) Practical blocks   Besides the many personal and organizational blocks to supervision, some people also face practical difficulties in getting the supervision that they need. These could be financial (I can't afford supervision), or geographical (living in a very isolated place) or availability (being head of an establishment and one's manager not having the specialized skills).

All these blocks require the supervisee to have an even higher degree of pro-activity and also to think laterally. Isolated therapists who work alone may have to look outside their own training to find a skilled practitioner of another orientation, but who is sympathetic enough to support the therapist in developing within his or her own style and school of work. Some geographically isolated therapists have arranged infrequent supervision with supervisors to whom they have to travel great distances, but have supplemented these visits with either correspondence or telephone calls.

In Chapter 8 we look at ways of setting up and conducting peer supervision and support groups. This can either be with a group of other similar practitioners in your area, or be a reciprocal arrangement with one other practitioner who is also in the position of not being able to get appropriate supervision within his or her organizational structure. We also give examples of how one can use professional organizations or training courses to provide a network within which to establish such peer supervision contracts.

(f) Cultural blocks   Another difficulty or block in receiving support or supervision has been referred to in the last chapter and in the quotes at the beginning of this chapter – namely the difficulty in receiving. To receive makes one potentially more vulnerable, exposes need. It is often felt to be safer to work with clients who have to express *their* needs and leave us safe in our roles of providing.

Although this might be a personal difficulty, it is certainly culturally reinforced. As we quoted in the last chapter, 'We have been brought up to deny our needs ... To need is to be dependent, weak; needing implies submission to another' (Hillman 1979). This attitude certainly is there in individuals and is strongly reinforced by work cultures. In Fineman's study (1985) of social workers when talking about the double standards of giving and not receiving he quotes one worker as saying:

> This is a particular caring group of people, but they play a charade with each other's problems and stresses. There's a sort of collusive arrangement not to talk to people about their stresses. If it's linked to a home situation there's a shame that they, as *social workers*, feel stressed ... No one stops to ask why this should be the case.

and continues:

> It was an odd feeling for those who found themselves facing, and contributing, to a wall of interpersonal evasiveness or even indifference inside the office, while professing just the opposite to clients outside the office ... They felt helpless victims of a climate which provided little of the emotional support they desired.

In this way a work culture might reinforce an individual's own inner feelings about asking for help; so, in spite of grumbling about lack of good supervision, there can be an unwillingness to really do something about it (see Chapter 11 on organizational cultures).

Here is part of an article from one of our supervisees who is a speech therapist. We have included it because she writes very clearly and openly about how her chosen profession's blocks around supervision reinforced her own, and because she demonstrates the changes she made to break her personal patterns. She also ends by asking some very relevant questions which do not only apply to speech therapists but all helping professions. You might try to answer these questions for yourself about your own work setting.

> As a disillusioned speech therapist who has considered leaving the profession several times I was interested to read that the majority of

speech therapists in full-time posts were mainly newly qualified, and those who have left the profession were mainly experienced full-timers. It struck me that these therapists had left without speaking out and saying why. Here is my story:

I started training at the age of 21. I knew that speech therapy was a small profession and that therapists were poorly paid. In fact I was already earning more than a senior speech therapist in my previous job in catering. However I liked working with people and had a genuine interest in communication problems. I wanted job satisfaction and felt that this would be more satisfying than a large salary.

I attacked my first job with a vigour and enthusiasm that I now recognize in many newly qualified therapists. I was keen to put into practice all that I had learnt. I was highly motivated. However, I should have begun listening to the messages behind the questions and comments I was receiving from other professionals, friends and relatives:

'Speech therapy must be a very lonely job.'
'Who do you go to for support?'
'Do you receive supervision?'
I can remember my replies were of the following nature:
'I like being my own boss.'
'I don't need support.'
'I am qualified and no longer need supervision.'

My first Senior 1 post, two years after qualifying, was very challenging. My job was divided between setting up an advisory speech-therapy service to a social services department and introducing speech therapy into a language unit which had been open for one year without a speech therapist. I felt I was appointed because I presented as a self-starter who could work without supervision and enjoyed challenges.

Even as I write this, a voice inside me is saying, 'What is wrong with that?' and 'Maybe you just don't have what it takes to be successful.' I have enough faith in myself to know these voices are wrong. If we do not question the assumptions or challenge the rationale behind such management decisions, we become guilty of perpetuating these fantasies. Being a self-starter often means taking up a post which has been poorly set up, then not being given the power to make necessary changes. I feel the personality of those attracted to the caring professions lends itself to exploitation and denial of their own needs. How many times have you heard 'We are here to help our patients.' This is, of course, what may have attracted us to our work, but at what price. The reverse side of the coin often appears to be 'My needs don't matter.'

Despite starting a counselling course, I still believed that I did not need support or require supervision. During the first year I refused to join a support group as it sounded too much like something found in a Californian suburb!

I found my new job very difficult and the team leader for the social-work team started questioning me on how much support I received. She was shocked when she realized I saw my line manager very infrequently. She suggested that she and I met fortnightly to discuss the job. These meetings became supervision, even though the team leader was not my line manager, and were very supportive.

Through discussing my work during these supervision sessions and through greater self-awareness, gained as a result of my counselling course, I began to realize that I was going through '*professional burnout*'. By this I mean that I had reached a point when I no longer had the enthusiasm to keep injecting into the job because I felt that my efforts were not effective or appreciated. The side effects of burnout for me were tiredness, lethargy, poor time-keeping and boredom. I had believed that I would always remain as highly motivated as I had been in my first job only four years ago.

The two things that kept me going through this period were supervision and *praise* (something we tend to give to the patients much more than to other staff). I feel I achieved a lot during this period, by learning how to use the support systems both on the course and at work.

After two years in this post I felt the need for a change. Where did I go from here? I decided to move into an area of work that had always interested me, 'speech therapy within psychiatry'. I found myself with another challenging post. After the initial excitement of the new job, etc. I realized I was back at the beginning of the long uphill struggle of getting a new service going.

There was no formal supervision or support system set up. The voice inside me said: 'Of course, you should be able to do this without support.' When I spoke about the difficulties of the post I heard the responses from others as criticism. I even found myself as saying the job was going well. It was difficult to admit, the therapist in me did not want to admit, that I could not cope. Eventually I called out for support. Then my overworked and, probably, unsupported GP also wanted to find a solution to my problem and put me on anti-depressants.

The speech-therapy profession is concerned about why so many experienced staff are leaving four or five years after being trained. I think my story illustrates one of the main reasons. Therapists who are working in the field need support and supervision. If they are not rewarded and valued by members of their own profession, what hope is there of receiving this from other professions and the government in the future?

I have thought about some questions that each speech therapist should ask before accepting a post:

- Does the district therapist see all new employees shortly after they commence and at regular intervals thereafter?

- Are there regular staff appraisals?
- Is there supervision for all staff members at all levels?
- Are support groups facilitated by an independent person encouraged?
- Are therapists encouraged to meet their colleagues regularly and is there provision made in the timetable for this?

Perhaps by identifying our needs and finding ways of getting them met, we will not have to take such drastic steps as leaving the profession.

(Geraldine Rose, unpublished work, 1987)

In the above article the writer was quite open about her own resistances as well as the profession's shortcomings. Good experiences of supervision enabled her to see what she was missing. She was not only lacking supervision, but until she went on the counselling course she was also lacking peer support. Even in social work where supervision is more acceptable, we think it is important that the worker receive good supervision *and* be in a supportive peer culture. Too much reliance on one individual supervisor can create unhealthy dependence.

In view of what has been written above about the various personal, interpersonal, practical and organizational blocks to getting supervision, you might like to return to the map of your own support system and review the blocks you experience. Awareness of the blocks is the first step in overcoming them and it is to this that we now turn.

Self-supervision

This is a form of supervision that is always relevant, even if you are receiving good supervision elsewhere. One aim of all supervision is to help practitioners develop a healthy internal supervisor which they can have access to while they are working.

An important aspect of self-supervision is to be able to reflect on one's own working. Borders and Leddick (1987) provide some very useful questions for such a reflection process.

Self-Observation (linking counsellor thoughts, feelings, actions with client behaviours)

(a) What was I hearing my client say and/or seeing my client do?
(a) What was I thinking and feeling about my observations?
(c) What were my alternatives to say or do at this point?
(d) How did I choose from among the alternatives?
(e) How did I intend to proceed with my selected response(s)?
(f) What did I actually do?

Self-Assessment (evaluating counsellor performance by observing client response)

(a) What effects did my response have on my client?
(b) How, then, would I evaluate the effectiveness of my response?

This reflection process can also be deepened by the supervisees' developing their own system of writing up the work they do, in a way that records not only the facts necessary for professional practice, but reflects on the process of the work and monitors our own body sensations, breathing, feelings, thoughts and actions, whilst with the client.

These written processes of reflection can be further deepened by using audio and visual tape-recording of work with clients and patients and developing ways of using these tapes to further one's own self-supervision. Kagan (1980) has done much to develop ways of learning through seeing tapes of ourselves working and we will be writing further about our own systems for self-supervision (Shohet, Hawkins and Wilmot forthcoming).

What is essential for all forms of self-supervision is giving oneself enough time and also being willing to confront one's own ways of working. Many of our trainees have found their first attempts to learn from listening to themselves on tape to be a painful and profoundly confronting experience.

Being pro-active within supervision

The need to be pro-active does not stop at the point where you have set up both a good support system and have found a good supervisor or supervisory situation. It is all too easy at this point to slide back into dependency and just accept the style and level of supervision that the supervisor provides. To ensure you get the supervision you want, you need to take full responsibility for your part in contracting and negotiating how the supervision will operate, what it will focus on and how the process will be monitored and reviewed.

Contracting Pat Hunt (1986) emphasizes the value of having a clear supervision contract: 'Supervision can become a more effective and satisfying activity for both supervisor and supervisee in any setting if there is a more *explicit* contract on what it is about.' She talks about the need for a 'supervisory alliance' and this includes:

> more openness and clarity on the methods to be used in supervision, and why they are used, the style of supervision, the goals of supervision, the kind of relationship it is hoped to achieve and the responsibilities of each partner in the supervisory relationship.

When contracting with your supervisor, it is important that both parties have the opportunity to say how they see the purpose of the sessions, explore how much their expectations match, and look at their hopes and fears concerning the working relationship. Where there is a mismatch in expectations, it is important that these differences are further explored and some form of negotiation takes place. As much as possible any conflict of purpose should be talked over, as should any issues of style, assumptions and values. Ground rules need to be established about frequency, duration and place and about how cases are to be brought; also how the supervision contract and the work will be reviewed and evaluated; finally, if relevant, what procedures there are for emergencies?

The need for such explicit contracting has been clearly expressed by Brigid Proctor (1988).

> If supervision is to become and remain a co-operative experience which allows for real, rather than token accountability, a clear – even tough – working agreement needs to be negotiated. The agreement needs to provide sufficient safety and clarity for the student or worker to know where she stands: and it needs sufficient teeth for the supervisor to feel free and responsible for making the challenges of assessments which belong with whatever role – managerial, consult-ative, or training – the context requires.

Evaluating your supervisor When exploring blocks to receiving supervision (see p. 22), we mentioned that one of the most common fears of supervisees is how they will be judged and evaluated by their supervisor. What most supervisees forget, or do not even consider, is that supervisors may also be anxious about how they are being judged or evaluated by their supervisees. Evaluation and review should be a two-way process and needs to be regularly scheduled into the supervision arrangements. This ensures that fears on both sides about 'how I am doing' can be brought into the open, and there is a chance to give clear feedback and, where necessary, to renegotiate the supervision contract.

Borders and Leddick (1987) provide a very useful check-list of 41 points for evaluating your supervisor. This list includes:

- helps me feel at ease with the supervision process;
- can facilitate and accept feedback from the supervisee;
- helps me clarify my objectives in working with clients;
- explains the criteria for any evaluation of my work, clearly and in behavioural terms;
- encourages me to conceptualize in new ways regarding my clients;
- enables me to become actively involved in the supervision process.

We would invite you to write your own evaluation criteria – some will be something you might ask of any supervisor and some might be of this particular supervisor at this particular time, related to the current work situation.

Supervisee responsibilities Brigid Proctor (1988) has drawn up a list of responsibilities for the student/supervisee. By terming them responsibilities, she points out that being more active in getting the right sort of supervision also involves more on-going responsibility. The responsibilities of the supervisee include:

- identify practices issue with which you need help and ask for help;
- become increasingly able to share freely;
- identify what responses you want;
- become more aware of the organizational contracts that affect supervisor, clients and supervisee;
- be open to feedback;
- monitor tendencies to justify, explain or defend;
- develop the ability to discriminate what feedback is useful.

In stressing the essential equality of the relationship we do not want to overlook the fact that in most supervisory relationships there is a managerial responsibility carried by the supervisor. The supervisee needs to be aware of this, and both parties need to work at integrating the managerial aspects of supervision so that they do not invalidate the opportunity for equality.

Finally we will conclude with some questions to help you consider ways of being more pro-active about your support and supervision:

- What are the strengths and weaknesses of your present support system? What do you need to do about improving it?
- How do you recognize that you are under stress? What ways do you use to alleviate this stress? Do these coping mechanisms provide just short-term relief, or do they change the cause of the stress?
- What are your specific needs from supervision and how far do your present supervisory arrangements meet them?
- Do you need to renegotiate the contract with your supervisor, supervision group or work team? Make as many of the transactions and assumptions as explicit as possible. Are all/both parties clear about the purpose of supervision?
- Are there additional forms of supervision (peer-supervision, etc.) that you need to arrange for yourself?
- How open do you feel to supervision and feedback? If not, are there personal changes you could make to open up the communication?
- Are you frightened of being judged and assessed? Have you tried checking out whether your fears are justified or fantasy?
- Can you confront your supervisor and give him or her feedback? If not, are the constraints internal or external?
- Are you stuck in blaming others for what you yourself can change? We often find on our courses that supervisees depower themselves, by having an investment in believing that they can not change what their supervisor or organization does to support them. When confronted on this, they have gone back and found that many more changes are possible than they previously believed.
- Do you carry some of your supervisor's anxieties, so that you have to look after them?
- Is it feasible to have a more equal relationship? How far is it appropriate and is it what you want, given that more equality means more responsibility?

PART TWO

Becoming a supervisor and the process of supervision

4 Becoming a supervisor

Supervising is new to me. It's OK, I suppose, but I'm anxious – I'm never quite sure whether I'm giving the people I'm supervising exactly what they are wanting. ... I'm really afraid about what they will say about me so I don't ask. To be judged by a colleague is just too much.

(Fineman 1985: 52)

Introduction

Suddenly becoming, or being asked to be, a supervisor, can be both exhilarating and daunting. Without training or support the task can be overwhelming. If you are reading this book, having just become a supervisor, we would encourage you not to start with this chapter, because as we mentioned in the previous chapter, you cannot expect to give good supervision unless you have first learnt how to receive supervision and be a pro-active supervisee.

Why be a supervisor?

There are many reasons why you might become or might have already become a supervisor. For some it is the natural progression that comes with promotion. They become nursing tutors, senior social workers or area youth officers, and discover that, instead of spending time seeing clients, for which they had been trained, they are now spending all their time seeing junior staff. Some counsellors or therapists find that they have become, over time, one of the most senior practitioners in their area, and supervisees start coming to them. Some staff find that they greatly miss the direct contact with clients and are nostalgic for their earlier days in the work. Such staff can be prone to turning their supervisees into substitute clients, to keep their hand in with therapeutic work.

Others turn to supervision to get away from the pressures of client work, in the false hope that seeing staff provides a quiet life! After several years as a helping professional they opt, not for a specialist post, but to go into student supervision or to become a tutor in their chosen profession. For some the role of supervisor does fit more easily than for others. They find themselves at home in a role that requires both personal development and educational skills.

Others get promoted into management because they are better administrators than they are at working with people, but unfortunately for such people and their organizations management positions in the helping professions nearly always include some supervision responsibilities. These staff then become the reluctant supervisors, who are always too busy with 'important meetings' and finishing 'essential reports' to see their supervisees.

Some staff are so able to arrange their work that they can mix some direct work with clients, with being a supervisor of others. We would recommend that wherever possible staff who supervise or teach should still be practising whatever they teach or supervise. It is all too easy to get out of touch with the realities of being at the 'coal-face' and to wonder why your supervisees are making such heavy weather of what seems perfectly straightforward from your perspective as supervisor. The mix of work can have advantages in both directions. Many new supervisors in several professions have remarked to us how having to supervise other staff helped them revitalize their own work with clients and start to think afresh about what they did themselves.

Many staff become and stay supervisors through being attracted to the challenge and scope of the role. Here is an account from a colleague.

> I feel most challenged and excited in supervision by the tension between the loving relationship and holding my own authority. Supervision is the place in my work where I can be at my most free-ranging – playful, free to think aloud, able to comment on the process, challenge, take a journey into the unknown. Then there is the opposite side when I really have to hold the boundaries, own my own authority and risk the good relationship for the sake of the truth. Each time this has happened, I have found it risky, self-challenging, lonely for a while, but also very mind-clearing and transformational and ultimately very strengthening to both ourselves and the relationship.

Being a supervisor provides an opportunity to develop one's educative skills in helping other staff to learn and develop within their work. As a new supervisor you are impelled to stop, reflect upon and articulate the ways you have worked as a practitioner, many of which you may have begun to take for granted. The challenge is then to use your own experience to help supervisees develop their own style of working and their own solutions to difficult work situations.

Another reason, which is often denied, for becoming a supervisor can be that of becoming one up on the other staff. Many of us will remember the joy when we entered our second year at a school – we were no longer the youngest or most gullible, there were now others we could tell 'what is what' to. New supervisors can be eager to mask their own anxieties by using their supervisees to bolster up their own pseudo-role of expert – the one who has all the answers.

Finally another hidden motive in giving supervision can be when staff who do not know how to get decent supervision for themselves can compensate by giving to other staff the sort of supervision they need and want for themselves, in the vain hope that this will magically lead to someone offering it to them.

Getting started

The first prerequisite for being a good supervisor is being able to actively arrange good supervision for yourself (see Chapter 3). A useful question to ask yourself is: 'Am I currently receiving adequate supervision, both for the other work I am doing and for being a supervisor?'

Before you give your first supervision sessions, we think it is useful for you to sit down and reflect on your own overt and covert motives that you bring to supervision. This is not in order to suppress the more shameful motives but to find some appropriate way to meet the needs the motives represent.

It would also be worthwhile to sit down and write out examples of positive and negative supervision experiences you yourself have received. What are your positive role models and what sort of supervisory experiences would you want to avoid repeating for your own supervisees?

Your expectations may well set the tone of what happens in the supervision sessions you give; if you go into them expecting them to be full of conflict or to be problematic they may well end up that way; if you go in expecting them to be interesting, engaging and co-operative, you may well produce the necessary climate that makes it that way.

Brigid Proctor (1988) suggests that it is most useful to start with the assumption:

that workers in the human service professions can be relied on

- to want to monitor their own practice;
- to learn to develop competence;
- and to respond to support and encouragement.

Starting with this basic assumption, even though at times it may not appear totally true, is helpful in setting a positive tone.

It is, however, possible that you are part of an organization where a negative culture about supervision has already developed, or where supervision is totally absent. You may find it supportive to recognize that some of the difficulties are not all yours and to read Chapters 11 and 12.

Qualities needed to be a good supervisor

Carifio and Hess (1987: 244) quote a variety of sources in looking at the qualities of the 'ideal supervisor' which they see as similar to the qualities of the ideal psychotherapist, but employed differently. These qualities include empathy, understanding, unconditional positive regard, congruence, genuineness (Rogers 1957); warmth and self-disclosure (Coche 1977); flexibility, concern, attention, investment, curiosity, and openness (Albott 1984; Aldridge 1982; Gittermann and Miller 1977; Hess 1980).

You will notice that most of these qualities, awareness and skills are ones you will already have or have developed in order to be a competent practitioner within the helping professions. Good counselling skills are a prerequisite for being a competent supervisor.

Brigid Proctor makes this point well when she says:

> The task of the supervisor is to help him (the supervisee) feel received, valued, understood on the assumption that only then will he feel safe enough and open enough to review and challenge himself, as well as to value himself and his own abilities. Without this atmosphere, too, he is unlikely to be open to critical feed-back or to pay good attention to managerial instructions.
>
> It will also be the case that a worker often comes to supervision stressed, anxious, angry, afraid. It is our assumption that only if he feels safe enough to talk about these uncomfortable feelings, and fully acknowledge then for himself will he be 'cleared' to re-evaluate his practice.
>
> (Proctor 1988)

As a supervisor you may recognize how relevant to this new task are the wealth and experience you have had as a practitioner. Some new supervisors need to be helped to adapt their useful counselling skills, to this new context; others hold on to their counselling skills too tenaciously and, as mentioned earlier, turn their supervisees into quasi-clients.

To start supervising you will first find it important to understand the boundaries of supervision and be able to make clear and mutually negotiated contracts. In Chapter 3, we discussed the importance of contracting clear supervision for the supervisee, and in Chapter 6 we will explore how the supervisor can manage this process. Many new supervisors are concerned about where supervision ends and therapy or counselling begins. Some new supervisors are anxious they will be flooded by their supervisees' personal problems. Others are only too eager to play therapist with their supervisee. Sometimes supervisees want to turn their supervisor into a 'quasi-therapist'.

When training therapists, one of us became aware that several of his own supervisees were half secretly wishing to have therapy with him rather than supervision. In exploring this further he became aware of another factor in this dynamic; that their wish for replacing the supervision of their work with the client with quasi-therapy for themselves was partly due to envy of their clients, to whom they were not only giving the attention in their therapy that they wished for themselves, but were having to give them yet more attention in the supervision. He began to realize that this envy needed to be made conscious and that the supervisees should be helped to look at what other forms of support they needed or wanted for themselves.

Kadushin (1968) describes a similar pattern in social work, when supervisees play the game of 'Treat me, don't beat me'. This game can be extremely alluring to the supervisor in several ways:

1. because the game appeals to the ... worker in him ... who is still interested in those who have personal problems. 2. because it appeals to the voyeur in him (many supervisors are fascinated by the opportunity to share in the intimate life of others). 3. because it is flattering to be selected as therapist, and 4. because the supervisor is not clearly certain as to whether such a redefinition of the situation is not permissible.

Good supervision inevitably focuses some of its attention on the dynamics of the supervisee, but this must always arise out of work-related issues and be done in the service of understanding and being able to manage the work better.

Second you need to develop your framework for supervising, which is appropriate to the setting in which you work. This framework needs to be clear enough to be explainable to your supervisees, but also flexible enough to be adapted to meet the changing needs of different supervisees, at different levels and with a variety of situations.

The most difficult new skill that supervision requires is what we call the 'helicopter ability'. This is the ability to switch perspectives; to be able to focus on the client that the supervisees are describing; to focus on the supervisees and their process; to be able to focus on your own process and the here and now relationship with the supervisees; to be able to see the client within their wider context and help the supervisees do likewise; and to see the work within the wider context of the organization and inter-organizational issues. This skill cannot be learnt before you start and indeed takes many years to develop. What is important is to know of the existence of all the possible levels and perspectives and then gradually to expand your focus within the sessions. However, do not try and get all the possible perspectives into every session, or your supervisees will get indigestion.

Finally, before we go on to present the different maps and models of supervision, we would like to spend some time looking at the complex roles that a supervisor has to combine. Clarifying your role(s) as supervisor is half the battle in achieving a clear framework.

Supervisor roles

As supervisor you have to encompass many functions in your role. In part you are a counsellor giving support; you are also an educator helping your supervisee learn and develop, and in many situations you are also a manager with responsibilities both for what the supervisee is doing with and to the client and also to the organization within which you both work. Several writers have looked at the complexity of roles that this provides for the supervisor (Bernard 1979; Hess 1980; Hawkins 1982; Holloway 1984; Ellis and Dell 1986; Carroll 1987). Among the sub-roles most often noted are:

- teacher
- monitor evaluator
- counsellor
- colleague
- boss
- expert technician

In our training course on social-work supervision we involve all the trainee supervisors in looking at the variety of helping relationships that they have experienced in their lives and the expectations and transactions that these roles involve. We ask them to brainstorm (for a description of brainstorming see p. 61) types of people they have gone to for help in their lives; what needs they take to these people and what they expect to receive. We end up with a list that typically looks like Table 4.1.

Table 4.1

Helping role	What you take to them	What you expect to receive
doctor	symptoms	diagnosis, cure
priest	sins, confessions	penitence, forgiveness
teacher	ignorance, questions	knowledge, answers
solicitor	injustice	advocacy
judge	crimes	retribution
friend	yourself	acceptance, listening ear
mother	hurts	comfort
car mechanic	mechanical failure	technical correction and servicing

When the roles are not clearly contracted for and defined in supervision, and to a lesser extent even when they are, supervisors and supervisees will fall back on other patterns of relating which may be one of the typical transactions mentioned above. It is possible to have *crossed, collusive* or *named* transactions.

A collusive transaction happens when you go to your supervisor expecting a reassuring mum and your supervisor obliging plays out that role by constantly telling you that everything is fine. Such a collusive transaction may feel good to both parties at the time, but would be unproductive as it would be feeding the neurotic needs of both parties rather than the needs of the supervision.

If on the other hand you went expecting a reassuring mum and your supervisor played judge, you would have a crossed transaction. In the latter case you would probably feel misunderstood and put down and that your supervisor was very unsupportive.

A named transaction is when one or other of the parties names the patterns and the games that are being played, so they become a choice rather than a compulsive process.

The supervisor has to be able to combine the roles of educator, supporter and at times manager, in an appropriate blend. As Hawthorne (1975) notes: 'It requires effort and experience to integrate these into a comfortable and effective identity.'

Much of the conflict around the role of the supervisor emerges from the difficulty that many supervisors have in finding an appropriate way of taking authority and handling the power inherent in the role. The rewarding aspect of this struggle was described earlier in this chapter (p. 34). Lillian Hawthorne (1975) has written about this difficult and yet crucial task:

> Many supervisors, especially new ones, have difficulty adjusting to their new authority. ... 'The balance which they have worked out for their personal lives between dominance and submission is upset by the new responsibility.' The supervisory relationship is complex, intense and intimate ... Sometimes the effort (to take on authority) is hampered by the supervisor's unfamiliarity with the requirements of his role, by difficulties stemming from personal experiences with authority, or by discomfort in the one-to-one relationship.

Hawthorne goes on to describe the sort of games supervisors play either to abdicate power or to manipulate power. Abdication games include:

- 'They won't let me': I would like to agree to what you are asking, *but* senior management won't let me.
- 'Poor me'; 'I'm sorry about having to cancel our weekly conferences, but you have no idea how busy I am with these monthly lists for the director.'
- 'I'm really a nice guy.' Look at how helpful and pleasant I am being to you.
- 'One good question deserves another.' How would you answer that question.

Manipulation of power games include:

- 'Remember who is boss.' Artificially asserting the power of one's role.
- 'I'll tell on you.' Threatening to pass on information about the supervisee to more senior management.
- 'Father or Mother knows best.' Acting in a parental or patronizing manner.
- 'I am only trying to help you.' Defending against criticism from the supervisee by pleading altruism.
- 'If you knew Dostoyevsky like I know Dostoyevsky' or showing off your knowledge to make the supervisee feel inferior.

In the next chapter we will go on to look at positive ways of combining the roles of educator, supporter and manager, and at taking the appropriate authority, depending on the experience of the supervisees and the supervision contract you have with them.

Conclusion

To be a supervisor is both a complex and enriching task. It is deceptively similar to, and uses the same sort of skills as practitioner work, but the supervisor must be clear about how it is different in content, focus and boundaries. It is also important to explore your feelings, motives and expectations of being in the role of supervisor, as they will have a large effect on the supervision climate that you set in the sessions.

Above all, supervision is a place where both parties are constantly learning and to stay a good supervisor is to return regularly to question, not only the work of the supervisee, but also what you yourself do as supervisor and how you do it.

5 Maps and models of supervision

In this chapter we want to pause and provide a theoretical background and framework for supervision. It is written particularly for new supervisors to help them take a broad survey of what supervision is, the various types, aspects and styles that are possible; so that they can identify their own style of supervision and then find the particular sort that is most appropriate for the supervisee and the setting within which they work. The chapter also covers the issues that a new or experienced supervisor needs to consider and provides the basis for thinking about what training you might need in supervision.

What is supervision?

Hess (1980) defines supervision as: 'a quintessential interpersonal interaction with the general goal that one person, the supervisor, meets with another, the supervisee, in an effort to make the latter more effective in helping people.' This is similar to the other most commonly used definitions of supervision by Loganbill, Hardy and Delworth (1982): 'an intensive, interpersonally focused, one-to-one relationship in which one person is designated to facilitate the development of therapeutic competence in the other person.'

The British Association of Counselling have recently been trying to create some ground rules for supervision. In their draft document on supervision (1987: 2) they also include an awareness of supervision being not only for the supervisee, but also for the benefit of the client. They state that 'The primary purpose of supervision is to protect the best interests of the client.'

But this is only the beginning of the story, because the task of supervision is not only to develop the skills, understanding and ability of the supervisee, but, depending on the setting, may have other functions. Kadushin (1976), writing about social work supervision, describes three main functions or roles, which he terms as *educative, supportive* and *managerial.*

Procter (undated), makes a similar distinction in describing the main processes in the supervision of counselling, for which she uses the terms *formative, restorative and normative.*

The educative or *formative* function, which is the one stressed in the definitions quoted above, is about developing the skills, understanding and abilities of the supervisees. This is done through the reflection on and exploration of the supervisees' work with their clients. In this exploration they may be helped by the supervisor to:

- understand the client better;
- become more aware of their own reactions and responses to the client;
- understand the dynamics of how they and their client were interacting;
- look at how they intervened and the consequences of their interventions;
- explore other ways of working with this and other similar client situations.

The *supportive* or *restorative* function is a way of responding to how any workers who are engaged in intimate therapeutic work with clients are necessarily allowing themselves to be affected by the distress, pain and fragmentation of the client and how they need time to become aware of how this has affected them and to deal with any reactions. This is essential if workers are not to become over full of emotions. These emotions may have been produced through empathy with the client or restimulated by the client, or be a reaction to the client. Not attending to these emotions soon leads to less than effective workers, who become either over-identified with their clients or defended against being further affected by them. This in time leads to stress and what is now commonly called 'burn out' (see Chapter 3). The British miners in the 1920s fought for what was termed 'pit-head time' – the right to wash off the grime of the work in the boss's time, rather than take it home with them. Supervision is the equivalent for those that work at the coal-face of personal distress, disease and fragmentation (see also Chapter 3).

The *managerial* or *formative* aspect of supervision provides the quality-control function in work with people. It is not only lack of training or experience that necessitates the need in us, as workers, to have someone look with us at our work, but our inevitable human failings, blind spots, areas of vulnerability from our own woundedness and our own prejudices. In many settings the supervisor may carry some responsibility for the welfare of the clients and how the supervisee is working with them. Supervisors may carry the responsibility to ensure that the standards of the agency in which the work is being done are upheld. Nearly all supervisors, even when they are not line managers, have some responsibility to ensure that the work of their supervisee is appropriate and falls within defined ethical standards.

Brigid Proctor (undated) gives some interesting vignettes to illustrate the different functions of supervision and to show how one can move from one to another.

A teacher in a young person's treatment centre is leaving after five demanding years. She asks for time to review the skills she has developed. It soon becomes clear that, before she can do that, she needs to talk about her feelings of loss and disorientation as she leaves the close, battering, intimate, structured environment. (*An apparently formative task becomes restorative.*)

A pregnancy adviser talks about her ethical and legal dilemmas in respect of a 15-year-old client. After giving her the 20 minutes she asked for, the group decides to spend all the following week's supervision on issues of confidentiality that arise in their work. (*A normative task.*)

A teacher in a disruptive unit starts to discuss a boy he is counselling. Through a socio-drama initiated by the supervisor the group helps him notice the complex system he and the boy are in and the different expectations placed on them both by parents, headmaster, social worker and others. At the end, he says he is clearer about his chosen task and role. (*Formative, normative and restorative.*)

In our work training supervisors we have elaborated the Kadushin supervisory functions, by listing what we see as the primary foci of social-work supervision, and relating these to the Kadushin categories.

Table 5.1 Primary foci of supervision

	Main categories of focus
To provide a regular space for the supervisees to reflect upon the *content* and *process* of their work	educational
To develop understanding and skills within the work	educational
To receive information and another perspective concerning one's work	educational/supportive
To receive both content and process feedback	educational/supportive
To be validated and supported both as a person and as a worker	supportive
To ensure that as a person and as a worker one is not left to carry, unnecessarily, difficulties, problems and projections alone	supportive
To have space to explore and express personal distress, restimulation, transference or counter-transference that may be brought up by the work	managerial/supportive
To plan and utilize their *personal* and *professional* resources better	managerial/supportive
To be pro-active rather than re-active	managerial/supportive
To ensure quality of work	managerial

Thus supervision has educative, supportive and managerial components, although in different settings some aspects will be more prominent than others and also the differing aspects are not totally separate but are combined in much of the supervisory focus. We have described elsewhere (Hawkins 1982) our own model that illustrates how these three areas are both distinct but also greatly overlap. A good deal of supervision takes place in the areas where managerial, supportive and educative considerations all intermingle.

Supervision contracts

It is important to form a clear contract for every supervisory relationship, and in this contract to decide what managerial, educative and supportive responsibilities the supervisor is carrying. The first step in contracting is to be clear which of the main categories of supervision is being requested by the supervisee and being offered by the supervisor and what sort of match or mismatch exists. The main categories are:

Tutorial supervision

In some settings the supervisor may have more of a tutor role, concentrating nearly entirely on the educative function, helping a trainee on a course explore his or her work with clients, where someone in the trainee's workplace is providing the managerial and supportive supervisory functions.

Training supervision

Here the supervision also emphasizes the educative function and the supervisees will be in some form of training or apprenticeship role. They may be student social workers on placement or trainee psychotherapists working with training clients. The difference from tutorial supervision is that here the supervisor will have some responsibility for the work being done with the clients and therefore carry a clear managerial or normative role.

Managerial supervision

We use this term where the supervisor is also the line manager of the supervisee. As in training supervision the supervisor has some clear responsibility for the work being done with the clients, but supervisor and supervisee will be in a manager-subordinate relationship, rather than a trainer-trainee one.

Consultancy supervision

Here the supervisees keep the responsibility for the work they do with their clients, but consult with their supervisor, who is neither their trainer/nor manager, on those issues they wish to explore. This form of supervision is for experienced and qualified practitioners.

So far we have described only supervision which is *vertical*, by which we mean a more experienced supervisor working with a less experienced supervisee. It is also possible to have *horizontal* supervision contracts, between supervisees of the same level. This will be addressed further in the chapter on group supervision when we consider peer-group supervision. It is also possible to have a one-to-one peer-supervision contract. This would normally be a form of consultancy supervision, but it may also have a peer-training element.

In forming the contract it is also necessary to be clear about the boundaries of the supervision. This includes the practical boundaries, such as the times, frequency, place, what might be allowed to interrupt or postpone the session, and clarification of any payment that is involved, etc.

Another boundary that often worries both supervisees and new supervisors is the boundary between supervision and counselling or therapy. Clearly working in depth in any of the helping professions can restimulate personal feelings, distress, anger or unhappiness. These feelings need to be shared and explored if the worker is going to be able to function well and learn from the re-stimulative event. To give an example from a youth club:

> A youth-club leader had spent a lot of time with a 14-year-old boy whose father had just died. He came to the supervision very angry about how the boy was receiving very little help at school. It gradually emerged that his own father left home when he was quite young and he had to support his mother emotionally, with very little outside help.

The basic boundary in this area is that supervision sessions should always start from exploring issues from work and should end with looking at where the supervisee goes next with the work that has been explored. Personal material should only come into the session if it is directly affecting, or being affected by, the work discussed; or if it is affecting the supervision relationship. Thus, in the above case, it would be important to explore how the youth-club leader's own personal material was being restimulated by the death of the young boy's father and how this was colouring his perspective on the boy's needs. If such an exploration uncovered more material than could be appropriately dealt with in the supervision, the supervisor may suggest that the worker might want to get counselling or other forms of support in exploring these personal feelings.

A supervision contract should also include clear boundaries concerning confidentiality. Confidentiality is an old chestnut which brings concern to many new supervisors. So many supervisors fall into the trap of saying or implying to the supervisees that everything that is shared in the supervision is confidential, only to find that some unexpected situation arises where they find it is necessary to share material from the supervision beyond the boundaries of the session.

Clearly this is more likely to be the case of training or managerial supervision, where the supervisor has an agency function and responsibility, of which the supervision is part. But even in consultancy supervision there are circumstances in which material from the session may be appropriately taken over the boundary. The consultant supervisor may feel a personal need for supervision on how he or she is supervising this worker. Another, although less likely, possibility is that, within the supervision, gross professional misconduct may be revealed which the supervisee refuses to take active responsibility to redress. The supervisor may feel ethically or legally incumbent to take action, informing appropriate authorities.

Thus, in contracting the appropriate confidentiality boundary for any form of supervision, it is inappropriate either to say everything is confidential that is shared here, or, as in the case of one supervisor we knew, to say nothing here is confidential. The supervisor should rather be clear what sort of information participants would need to take over the boundary of the relationship; in what circumstances; how they would do this; and to whom they would take the information. Clearly every possible situation cannot be anticipated, but by such a general exploration the possibility of sudden betrayal is diminished.

We also give our supervisees the undertaking that we will treat everything they share with us in a professional manner and not gossip about their situation.

The contracting should also include some form of sharing of mutual expectations. What sort of style of supervising the supervisees most want and which of the possible foci do they wish the supervisor to concentrate on. The supervisors also need to state clearly what their preferred mode of supervising is, and any expectations they have of the supervisees. Do they expect the supervisees to bring written-up case notes or verbatim accounts of sessions? Do they require the supervisees to check with them or inform them whenever they take on a new client?

Before leaving the area of contracting, we would like to mention the issue of supervisory ethics. Most professional associations have codes of conduct and statements of ethics which stipulate the boundaries of appropriate behaviour between a worker and a client or patient and also provide the right of appeal for the client against any possible inappropriate behaviour by the worker. Very few professions are as clear about their code of practice for supervision. We do not want to prescribe what we think are appropriate ethical standards for supervisors, because this must invariably vary from one setting to another. However, we do consider it imperative that all new supervisors check whether there are ethics statements covering supervision within their profession and/or organization. If no such statement exists, we suggest that you review the ethical standards for work with clients and become clear within yourself which of them you feel apply to the supervision context. It is important that all supervisors are clear about the ethical boundaries of their supervisory practice and are able to articulate these to their supervisees.

Supervision modes

So far we have concentrated on contracts for formal one-to-one supervision, however, it is also possible to have supervision arrangements that are more informal or ad hoc. In some residential or day-care agencies much of the supervision will be outside formal individual sessions. Payne and Scott (1982) have produced a format for recognizing the choices between formal and informal; planned and *ad hoc* supervision. This is very useful in helping teams to recognize that a great deal of supervision happens in times and places other than those officially designated for supervision. Once this is recognized, the quality of the informal or *ad hoc* supervision can also be negotiated and improved. But first a word of warning. Although there is a lot of creative scope for more informal types of supervision, it is easy to use these less structured types of supervision to avoid the rigours and concentrated focus of regular, formal individual sessions. We have talked extensively in this book about the natural resistances and defences to both giving and receiving supervision, and without a formal structure these resistances can produce a lot of avoidance behaviour from both the supervisor and the supervisee. It is easy to create a climate where supervision is only requested when you have a recognizable problem and at other times you have to be seen to 'soldier on'. The dangers of this type of culture are explored more fully in Chapter 11.

Supervisory styles

Having looked at the various functions and modes of supervision, we will now look at how the style of supervision can vary within each of these different types. In this chapter we will provide you with a broad-brush distinction between different supervisory styles and then in the following chapter present our own model for more finely delineating and developing your own supervisory style.

One's style as a supervisor is affected by the style of one's practitioner work. If you are a Rogerian counsellor it is most likely that your style of supervision will be non-directive and supervisee-centred (see Rice, Chapter 12 of Hess 1980). If your training has been psychoanalytic, as a supervisor you may tend to concentrate on understanding the unconscious processes of the client or the supervisee (see Moldawsky, Chapter 11 of Hess 1980). If you are trained as a behaviourist, then as a supervisor you will tend to concentrate on client behaviour and the methodology of the worker (see Linehan, Chapter 13 of Hess 1980). It is also possible to integrate several different therapeutic approaches into one's own supervision style and this is explored by Boyd (1978).

Sometimes we are asked whether you should always ensure that your supervisor has the same type of training as the supervisee. There is no easy answer to this question, but both supervisor and supervisee need to share enough of a common language and belief system to be able to learn and work together. Sometimes having a supervisor with a very different training means that he or she is more able to see what your own belief system is editing out.

Supervisory style is also greatly affected by your own gender, age and cultural background, as well as your personality. It is important to be aware how these all affect the way you will view both the supervisees and the clients they will present to you. This is especially relevant when there is a match between the age, gender and background of the worker and the supervisor, but the client has a different age, background or gender, e.g. if the client is an old working-class, West Indian man, and the worker and supervisor are both young middle-class, white women. In such cases the supervisor has to work doubly hard to help the supervisee explore how her own background and attitudes are affecting how she sees and works with the client.

Ekstein (1969) offers a simple way of thinking about such issues, through considering our *blind spots, deaf spots* and *dumb spots*. Dumb spots are those where supervisees or supervisors are ignorant about what it is like to be in the position of the client. They lack the experience to understand what it means to be a homosexual; frightened of parental disapproval; or a member of an oppressed ethnic group. Blind spots are where the supervisee's own personal patterns and processes get in the way of seeing the client clearly (see the discussion of counter-transference in Chapter 6, mode 4). Deaf spots 'are those where the therapist not only cannot hear the client, but cannot hear the supervisor either. These are likely to involve particularly defensive reactions based on guilt, anxiety or otherwise unpleasant and disruptive feelings. Or hostility to authority figures' (Rowan 1983).

A developmental approach to supervision

In the sudden upsurge of literature on supervision in the field of counselling psychology in the United States, the main model that has emerged is the developmental approach. This approach suggests that supervisors need to have a range of styles and approaches which are modified as the counsellor gains in experience and enters different definable developmental stages.

One of the first seminal works in this field was by Hogan (1964) working in the field of training psychologists as psychotherapists. Many writers have followed since then; most notably Worthington (1987) and Stoltenberg and Delworth (1987). Rather than describe each of these models (they are well described in Stoltenberg and Delworth 1987: 18–30) we will integrate them into a combined developmental model of four major stages of supervisee development.

Level I

The first stage is characterized by trainee dependence on the supervisor. The supervisees can be anxious, insecure about their role and their own ability to fulfil it, lacking insight, but also highly motivated. A recent study by Hale and Stoltenberg (forthcoming) suggests that the two main causes of anxiety of new trainees is firstly evaluation apprehension and secondly objective self-awareness. Objective self-awareness is a term borrowed from social psychology and is used to suggest that 'the process of being videotaped, audiotaped, or otherwise made to focus on oneself ... can elicit negative evaluations of one's performance and concomitant feelings of anxiety' (Stoltenberg and Delworth 1987: 61).

New trainees have not had the experience to develop grounded criteria on which to assess their performance and consequently can feel very dependent on how their supervisor is assessing their work. This apprehension may be linked to the supervisor having some formal assessment role in their training or in their work evaluation, but will also be present on a more day-to-day basis in concern about how the supervisor is viewing their work, and how they compare to other supervisees that their supervisor sees.

We have found this concern to be present even when taping sessions is not employed, but where trainees are asked to bring 'verbatims' or accounts of sessions. Indeed all good supervision must help the supervisee to reflect back on themselves, and for the new trainee this is inevitably anxiety provoking.

Level I workers tend

> to focus on specific aspects of the client's history, current situation, or personality assessment data to the exclusion of other relevant information. Grand conclusions may be based on rather discreet pieces of information.
>
> (Stoltenberg and Delworth 1987: 56)

It is difficult for workers in this stage to have an overview of the whole therapeutic process as they have usually only worked with clients in the early stages of therapeutic work. This may make them impatient or fearful that the process will ever move on from a current sticking place.

In order to cope with the normal anxiety of Level I trainees, the supervisor needs to provide a clearly structured environment which includes positive feedback and encouragement to the supervisees to return from premature judgement of both the client and themselves to attending to what actually took place. 'Balancing support and uncertainty is the major challenge facing supervisors of beginning therapists' (Stoltenberg and Delworth: 64).

Level II

Here the supervisees have overcome their initial anxieties and begin to fluctuate between dependence and autonomy; and between over-confidence and being overwhelmed.

We have written elsewhere (Hawkins 1980) about how this stage manifests itself in residential workers in therapeutic communities. This paper, entitled 'Between Scylla and Charybdis', describes how the staff trainee has to be supported by tutors and supervisors to steer a course between submergence and over-identification representing the Charybdis on the one side and flight into over-professionalism being the Scylla on the other side. This is how a staff member disappearing into the Charybdis whirlpool was described:

the staff member stops reading books or writing letters; he becomes unable to objectify his experience in case conferences or supervision; he finds it difficult to set limits, say no to residents (clients) or to protect his off-duty hours ... unable to separate other people's difficulties from one's own intra-psychic dynamics, or investing one's own success or failure and validation in the success or failure of the residents.

(Hawkins 1980: 195)

The staff member who is dashed on the rocks of Scylla becomes

defensively over-clinical to avoid any personal involvement ... staff trainees become unable to meet clients on a person-to-person basis, desperately hold on to a false persona of adequacy and retreat into administration.

(Hawkins 1979: 222–3)

In their work with clients the Level II trainee begins to be less simplistic and single focused both about the development process of the client and their own training:

the trainee begins to realize, on an emotional level, that becoming a psychotherapist (*or other helping professional*) is a long and arduous process. The trainee discovers that skills and interventions effective in some situations are less than effective at other times.

(Stoltenberg and Delworth 1987: 71. We have inserted the italics section.)

Loss of the early confidence and simplicity of approach may lead some trainees to be angry with their supervisor whom they see as responsible for their disillusionment. The supervisor is then seen as 'an incompetent or inadequate figure who has failed to come through when he or she was so badly needed' (Loganbill, Hardy and Delworth 1982: 19).

Some writers have likened this stage of development to that of adolescence in normal human development, with Level I being similar to childhood; Level III early adulthood; and Level IV being full maturity.

Certainly Level II can feel to the supervisor like parenting an adolescent. There is testing out of one's authority, a fluctuation in moods and a need to provide both space for the trainees to learn from mistakes and a degree of holding and containment. In this stage the trainees can also become more reactive to their clients, who, like the supervisor, may also be felt as the cause of their own turbulence.

The supervisor of Level II trainees needs to be less structured and didactic than with Level I trainees, but a good deal of emotional holding is necessary as the trainees may oscillate between excitement and depressive feelings of not being able to cope, or perhaps even of being in the wrong job.

Level III

The Level III trainee shows increased professional self-confidence, with only conditional dependency on the supervisor. He or she has greater insight and shows more stable motivation. Supervision becomes more collegial, with sharing and exemplification augmented by professional and personal confrontation.

(Stoltenberg and Delworth 1987: 20)

The Level III trainee is also more able to adjust their approach to clients to meet the individual and particular needs of that client at that particular time. They are also more able to see the client in a wider context and have developed what we call 'helicopter skills'. These are the skills of being fully present with the client in the session, but being able simultaneously to have an overview that can see the present content and process in the context of:

the total process of the therapeutic relationship;
the client's personal history and life patterns;
the client's external life circumstances;
the client's life stage, social context and ethnic background.

It is less possible to recognize what orientation the trainee has been schooled in, as they have by this stage incorporated the training into their own personality, rather than using it as a piece of learnt technology.

Level IV

This stage is refered to as 'Level III integrated' by Stoltenberg and Delworth. By this time the practitioner has reached 'master' level 'characterized by personal autonomy, insightful awareness, personal security, stable motivation and an awareness of the need to confront his or her own personal and professional problems' (Stoltenberg and Delworth:

20). Often by this stage supervisees have also become supervisors themselves and this can greatly consolidate and deepen their own learning. Stoltenberg and Delworth (1987: 102) quote a colleague: 'When I'm supervising, I'm forced to be articulate and clear about connections across domains and that makes it easier for me to integrate.'

We often find that we say things to our supervisees that we need to learn. It is as if our mouth is more closely linked to our sub-conscious knowing than was our mental apparatus! Mulla Nasrudin, when he was asked how he had learnt so much, replied: 'I simply talk a lot and when I see people agreeing, I write down what I have said.'

Certainly the stage of Level IV is not about acquiring more knowledge, but allowing this to be deepened and integrated until it becomes wisdom; for as another Sufi teacher put it: 'Knowledge without wisdom is like an unlit candle.'

It is possible to compare the developmental stages of supervisee development to other developmental approaches. We have already mentioned the analogy to the stages of human growth and development. We can also posit the analogy to the stages of development within the medieval craft guilds. Here the trainee started as a *novice*, then became a *journeyman*, then an *independent craftsman*, and finally a *master craftsman*.

The model also has parallels in the stages of group development. Schutz (1973) describes how groups begin with the predominant concerns being *inclusion/exclusion*: can I fit in and belong here? Once this has been resolved the group will normally move on to issues of *authority*; challenging the leader, dealing with competitiveness, etc. Only then will the group move on to look at issues of *affection* and intimacy; how to get close to the others and what is the appropriate closeness. This progression of themes seems to be paralleled in the supervision-developmental approach, particularly where supervision is part of a training which is being carried out with other trainees (see also Chapter 9).

Finally the four stages can be seen as characterized by where the centre of their focus and concern is located (Table 5.2).

Table 5.2

Level I	self-centred	'Can I make it in this work?'
Level II	client-centred	'Can I help this client make it?'
Level III	process-centred	'How are we relating together?'
Level IV	process-in-context-centred	'How do processes interpenetrate?'

We will return to this map in the following chapter when we explore the developmental aspects of our own model of supervision.

Reviewing the developmental approach

The developmental model is a useful tool in helping supervisors more accurately to assess the needs of their supervisees and to realize that part of the task of supervision is to help in the development of the supervisee, both within stages and between stages of development. The model also stresses that as the supervisee develops so must the nature of the supervision.

However, there are limits to its usefulness that must be borne in mind. First, there is a danger of using the model too rigidly as a blueprint for prescribing how every supervisee at each stage should be treated, without enough reference to the particular needs of the individual, the style of the supervisor and the uniqueness of the supervisor-supervisee relationship.

Second, Hess (1987) points out that supervisors are also passing through stages in their own development and we must therefore look at the interaction of both parties' development stages. This challenge is taken up in part by Stoltenberg and Delworth (1987: 152-67).

Carroll (1987) warns those working outside America of another of the limitations of this model, which is that it has been developed entirely within an American context and

> We need to be careful that we do not transport theories that work well in other climates to Britain without serious investigation that they will adapt well to the changing environment. Counselling supervision may not be a good traveller.

He quotes the research by O'Toole (1987) which shows significant differences between the counselling climates in America and Britain. In the fields of psychotherapy and social work there are also major differences between the cultures on each side of the Atlantic.

Finally, we would do well to remember that we can become egotistic, over-inflated, in thinking that we are responsible for another person's development. Here is a story that beautifully makes this point.

> A man once saw a butterfly struggling to emerge from its cocoon, too slowly for his taste, so he began to blow on it gently. The warmth of his breath speeded up the process all right. But what emerged was not a butterfly but a creature with mangled wings.

Despite these reservations, we would particularly recommend some acquaintance with this model to all supervisors who work in the context of a training course, be it for nurses, social workers, counsellors or psychotherapists, in order that they may plan what supervision is most appropriate for trainees in different stages of the course.

Choosing your framework

Our hope is that this chapter will provide readers with the tools to choose and/or clarify:

- the supervision framework they wish to use;
- how they will amend their basic framework depending on the work, needs and developmental stage of the supervisee;
- how they will balance the competing demands of the educative, supportive and managerial functions of supervision;
- what sort of supervision contract they will negotiate, and what issues it will include.

However, the map is not the territory. Before setting off on an expedition into new terrain, you need to ensure that the map is as good as you can get, but once you have embarked on the journey you do not want to spend the whole time buried in your map. You only need the map to send you in the right direction, or to redirect you when you get lost and also to make periodic checks that you are all going in the right direction.

Finally, it is important that the map you develop is accessible to and understandable by your supervisees. Supervision is a joint journey and works best where there is a shared model and framework.

6 A process model of supervision

This chapter is written particularly for those who supervise counsellors or psychotherapists, but we hope it will also be of interest to those in other helping professions who supervise in-depth casework. Because of this focus we have used the term 'therapist' for the supervisee throughout this chapter. When reading this, it is possible to substitute the term worker, counsellor, social worker, psychiatrist, etc.

Having presented, in the previous chapter, the main maps and models of supervision that are currently available, we now turn to our own model of the supervision process. Our double matrix model, which we first presented in 1985 (Hawkins 1985), differs significantly from the other ways of looking at supervision. In this model we turn the focus away from the context and the wider organizational issues (discussed in the models in the previous chapter) to look more closely at the process of the supervisory relationship.

Our interest in this dimension began when we were trying to understand the significant differences in the way each member of our own peer group supervised and the different styles of supervision that we had encountered elsewhere. These differences could not be explained by developmental stages, our primary tasks, or our intervention styles. From further exploration came the realization that the differences were connected to the constant choices we were making, as supervisors, as to what we focused on.

At any time in supervision there are many levels operating. At a minimum all supervision situations involve at least four elements:

A supervisor

A supervisee

A client

A work context

Of these four, normally only the supervisor and the supervisee are directly present in the supervision session, except in live supervision. However, the client and the work context are carried into the session in both the conscious awareness and the unconscious sensing of the supervisee. They may also, at times, be brought indirectly into the session in the form of audio/video tapes or written verbatims of sessions or through role-play.

Thus the supervision process involves two interlocking systems or matrices: the therapy system which interconnects the client and the therapist through some agreed contract, regular time spent together and a shared task; and the supervision system or matrix which involves the therapist and the supervisor through their agreed contract, time spent together and shared task. The task of the supervisory matrix is to pay attention to the therapy matrix, and it is in how this attention is given that supervisory styles differ.

Our model divides supervision styles into two main categories:

- supervision that pays attention directly to the therapy matrix, through the supervisee and the supervisor, reflecting together on the reports, written notes or tape recordings of the therapy sessions;
- supervision that pays attention to the therapy matrix through how that system is reflected in the here-and-now experiences of the supervision process.

Each of these two major styles of managing the supervision process can be further subdivided into three categories, depending on the emphasis of the focus of attention. This gives us six modes of supervision as follows.

I   The therapy session is reported and reflected upon in the supervision

1   Reflection on the content of the therapy session

Attention is concentrated on the actual phenomena of the therapy session; how the clients presented themselves, what they chose to share, which area of their life they wanted to explore, and how this session's content might relate to content from previous sessions. The aim and goal of this form of supervision are to help the therapist pay attention to the client, the choices the client is making and the relatedness of the various aspects of the client's life.

2   Exploration of the strategies and interventions used by the therapist

The focus here is on the choices of intervention made by the therapist; not only what interventions were used but also when and why they were used. Alternative strategies and interventions might then be developed and their consequences anticipated. The main goal of this form of supervision would be to increase the therapist's choices and skills in intervention.

Figure 6.1

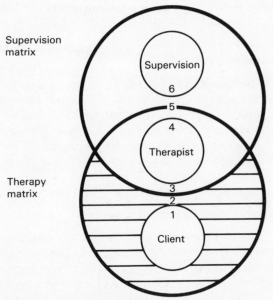

Supervision
matrix

Therapy
matrix

Note: Shaded area is only available to the supervision matrix through some form of reflection

3 Exploration of the therapy process and relationship

Here the supervisor will pay particular attention to what was happening consciously and unconsciously in the therapy process; how the session started and finished; what happend around the edges; metaphors and images that emerged; and changes in voice and posture. The main goal of this form of supervision will be the therapist having greater insight and understanding of the dynamics of the therapy relationship.

II Focus on the therapy process as it is reflected in the supervision process

4 Focus on the therapist's counter-transference

Here the supervisor concentrates on whatever is still being carried by the therapist, both consciously and unconsciously, from the therapy session and the client. The counter-transference may be of four different kinds: personal material of the therapist that has been re-stimulated by the therapy session; the transferential role that the therapist has been altercasted into by the client; the therapist's unconscious attempt to 'counter' the transference of the client; projected material of the clients that the therapist has taken in somatically, psychically or mentally (see also Casement 1985: 92–3).

5   Focus on the here-and-now process as a mirror or parallel of the there-and-then process

Here the supervisor focuses on the relationship in the supervision session in order to explore how it might be unconsciously playing out or paralleling the hidden dynamics of the therapy session (Mattinson 1975; Searles 1955). Thus, if the client was covertly acting in a passive–aggressive way to the therapist, this might emerge in the supervision by the therapist's becoming unconsciously passive–aggressive to the supervisor as they discuss that particular client.

6   Focus on the supervisor's counter-transference

Here the supervisor primarily pays attention to their own here-and-now experience in the supervision; what feelings, thoughts and images the shared therapy material stirs up in them. The supervisor uses these responses to provide reflective illumination for the therapist. The unconscious material of the therapy session which has been unheard at the conscious level by the therapist may emerge in the thoughts, feelings and images of the supervisor.

It would be very unusual to find a supervisor who remained entirely in one of these six modes of supervision and we would hold that good supervision must inevitably involve the movement between modes. However, distinguishing between the modes in their pure form has many advantages. It allows supervisors to be clearer about their own style, its strengths and weaknesses and which possible modes of supervision they might be avoiding out of habit or lack of familiarity and practice.

Not only does the model provide a way of increasing the options for the supervisor, but it also can be used by the supervisee as a language within which to negotiate changes in supervision style and can be used as a tool in a regular review and appraisal of the supervision.

The model can also be used to train supervisors in the various elements of the supervision process, learning the refinements of each focus separately, so that they can then develop their own style and method of putting the different processes together (see next chapter).

It is this approach that we use on our training course for those who supervise counsellors and therapists. We present each focus in detail and then provide a specific training exercise designed to train the course members in that particular style. (These exercises will be published separately in a training manual.) We liken this to musicians learning to play scales before performing concert pieces.

We will now look at each of the processes in more detail, taking you through them as if you were on supervisor training course.

Mode One: The content of the supervision session

> It is the task of the Supervisor to enable the supervisee to become more aware of what actually takes place in the session.
>
> (Shainberg 1983)

To a supervisor, focusing on what actually happened to the supervision session may sound deceptively easy. But as Shainberg points out in her excellent paper, 'Teaching therapists how to be with their clients', the difficulty for therapists in staying with their not knowing what is happening, and what to do in the therapy session, causes them to fear this relative impotence and rush to make premature sense. This can lead on to premature theorizing and over early interpretation of what has happened. Supervisors can both collude and intensify this process with their own anxiety and need to be potent and have answers for their supervisee.

Shainberg is not the first to point out this phenomenon. Freud relates how 'a store of ideas is created, born from a man's need to make his helplessness tolerable' (Freud 1927: 18) and Bion in his writings on therapy constantly entreats us to stay empty with our unknowing, uncluttered by premature judgement, theory and interpretation. 'In every consulting room there ought to be two rather frightened people' (Bion 1974). 'True knowing', Shainberg writes, comes from 'being able to observe and describe what is going on in the present in accurate, concrete, and complete detail. This is different from wanting to change or get rid of or compare or assume a fixed meaning about what is happening.' (Shainberg 1983: 164)

The first task in every supervisory exploration of clients is to have the therapists accurately describe the clients; how they came to be having therapy; their physical appearance; how they move and hold themselves; how they breathe, speak, look, gesture, etc; their language, metaphors and images and the story of their life as they told it.

The task requires the clear focus of a portrait painter or Zen archer and the supervisor's job is to help the supervisees to stay with this difficult task. This involves challenging the assumptions that the supervisees make and asking them to return to what they saw or what the client said. It also entails watching for the supervisees' 'ideological editor' or belief system that edits what information the supervisees are relating and forms the shape in which they present the clients.

Shainberg shows, in her paper, how often new therapists have a fixed notion of how the therapy should go. They are anxious to apply the theory that they have learnt about personality types and pathology to the patients they see before them. This leads them to stop seeing the actuality of the unique human being that they are with and can lead to 'objectification': the seeing of the patient as a challenge to their therapeutic prowess. In the second of her two illustrations Shainberg describes the 'objectification process' in one of her supervisees:

> She then said she did not experience the patient in the same way as she

would 'a fellow human being'. She could not feel other than that the patient was 'so far a test of my being a therapist'. I said she had turned the patient into an object 'to be worked on' at this point. She said she felt the gist of it was that 'if *it* is a person you can feel free, but if *it* is a patient you have to do something to change things. Otherwise what are you doing there?' I did not comment on the use of her word *it* but heard it as how remote she experienced the patient at this point from herself, as though the patient were not her fellow being sharing the human condition of suffering, daily conflict, having a mother and a father, being in fear, facing the inevitability of death.

(Shainberg 1983: 168)

Shainberg gradually helps supervisees become aware of the internal dialogue inside their own heads, the judgements, expectations, self-doubt, etc., so that they can return to the actuality of the experience of *being* with the patient prior to *doing*.

Focus all your attention on seeing as clearly as you can the way this person behaves and what you think and feel being with her. Do not try to find meanings, make connections, or understand. Observe what takes place and your responses.

(Shainberg 1983: 169)

There is a place for theorizing and using theory to understand what is happening in work with clients, but it must always come after direct encounter with the client in the fullness of their unique being. Between the stage of concentrating on the direct observation and the content of what the client said and turning to theoretical consideration, there are several further steps that need to be taken. As Shainberg has already said, the next stage is to attend to the feelings of the supervisee while being with the patient and this we will talk about more when we look at Mode Three.

After that there are further stages of content focus. There is the exploration of the connections of the content of one part of the session with material from elsewhere in the session, listening for the whole that is contained within each of the parts.

Then there is the tentative linking of material from one session to material and sequences from previous sessions. Beginning therapists so often treat each session as if it was a closed system, rather than part of an on-going process.

Working further out, we can then explore the links of the content to the life of the patient outside therapy and also prior to their therapy. In this we can look at the content in the therapy session as a microcosm of the macrocosm of the client's life as a whole.

In focusing on content there are two useful additional processes. One is to concentrate on attending to the first five minutes of the session; to see how the clients first presented and revealed themselves before the dyadic process got fully under way.

The other useful approach is to use video or audio recordings of sessions.

Here one can move between the actuality of the material and the feelings of the therapist. (See Kagan 1980 and Shohet, Hawkins and Wilmot forthcoming.)

Mode Two: Focusing on strategies and interventions

In this mode the supervisor focuses on what interventions the supervisees made in their work with the clients, how and why they made them and what they would rather have done. One psychotherapy trainer that we interviewed uses this approach as the main focus of her supervision:

> I ask them what interventions they have made? What reasons they had for making them? Where their interventions were leading them? How they made their interventions and when? Then I ask what do you want to do with this client now?
>
> (Davies 1987)

It is useful to bear in mind Abraham Maslow's aphorism: 'If the only tool you have is a hammer, you will tend to treat everything as if it is a nail' and it is important to make sure that your supervisees not only have a wide range of interventions in their tool box, but also that they use the tools appropriately and are not blunting their chisels by using them to turn screws!

We have often found that in thinking how to work with a client, therapists can get stuck in dualistic thinking. They will make statements which we term 'Either-or-isms' such as:

> I either have to confront his controlling behaviour or put up with it.

> I didn't know whether to wait a bit longer, or interpret his silence as his aggression towards me.

> I don't know whether to continue working with him.

As you can see they do not always contain the words 'either–or', but they are always based on the supervisees' seeing two opposing options. The job of the supervisor is to avoid the trap of helping the supervisees evaluate between these two choices, but to point out how they have reduced numerous possibilities to only two. Once the supervisees have realized that they are operating under a restrictive assumption, the supervisor can help them generate new options for intervening.

Generating new options can be done by using a simple brainstorming approach. The basic rules of brainstorming are:

- Say whatever comes into your head.
- Get the ideas out. Don't evaluate or judge the ideas.
- Use the other person's ideas as springboards.
- Include the wildest options you can invent.

Brainstorming is helped by setting a high target for options, for it is only when we have exhausted all the obvious rational choices that the creative unconscious starts to get going. Often it is the craziest idea that contains the kernel of a creative way forward. In a group supervision you could try brainstorming twenty ways of dealing with a therapeutic impasse: in individual supervision you could ask the supervisee to invent six or seven different ways of handling the situation with which they are supposedly stuck.

Group supervision offers this mode of supervision many creative possibilities. The group contains a greater variety of styles and can avoid the dualism in the dyadic system where there is either the supervisor's or the supervisee's approach.

In group supervision there is also a greater range of active role-playing possibilities. Different group members can choose one possible approach they would like to try out from the list of brainstormed possibilities. Then with the supervisee playing the client, several different interventions and strategies can be tried and evaluated (see Chapter 8). Even in individual supervision the supervisee can try out different interventions. It is possible to use an empty chair or the supervisor to represent the client. If necessary, after trying the intervention, they can role-reverse and respond to the intervention from within the role of the client.

Many supervisors, when focusing on therapeutic interventions, would offer their own intervention. There are dangers in doing this. It is easy as supervisor to want to show off your therapeutic skill without fully acknowledging how much easier it is to be skilful in the relative ease of the supervisory setting than when face to face with the client. The other danger is that the interventions of the supervisor will be introjected (swallowed whole) by the supervisees rather than helping them to develop their own improved interventions.

In the following chapter on training supervisors we will describe John Heron's classification of interventions which divides all forms of possible interventions into six categories. We point out how there is no value judgement that one intervention is better than another, but that all interventions can be used, *appropriately*, *degenerately* or *perversely*. We would do this in order that supervisors may look at which forms of intervention they compulsively use and which they mostly avoid using. From this they can discover some aspects of the strength and weakness of their style, and how they might want to change the balance in the sort of interventions they are using.

We find that monitoring our own interventions in such a way sharpens our awareness of the interventions of our supervisees.

There is a whole school of Strategic Therapy which is mainly used for working with families and utilizes a whole range of specific live supervision techniques, with the supervisor delivering strategic interventions to the therapist, often from behind a one-way mirror, through an earpiece or telephone. Focusing on strategy should not be confused with 'strategic' approaches to therapy, for all therapists use some form of strategy, be it interpretation, reflection, silence or the active facilitation of bodywork.

Mode Three: Focusing on the therapy process

In this mode the focus is neither on the client, nor the supervisee, nor their interventions, but on the system that the two parties create together. In this mode the supervisor focuses on the conscious and unconscious interaction between therapist and client. To start with the supervisor might ask one or more of the following:

- What is the history of the relationship?
- How did you meet?
- How and why did this client choose you?
- What did you first notice about this client?
- Tell the story of the history of your relationship?

These questions must clearly be requesting something different from a case history and must help the supervisee to stand outside the therapy relationship in which they might be enmeshed or submerged and see the pattern and dynamic of the relationship.

Other techniques and questions that encourage this distancing and detachment are:

Find an image or metaphor to represent the relationship.

Imagine what sort of relationship you would have, if you and the client met in other circumstances, or if you were both cast away on a desert island.

Become a fly on the wall in your last therapy session; what do you notice about the relationship?

These are all techniques to help the supervisees to see the relationship as a whole rather than just stay with their own perspective from within the relationship. But it is the supervisor's job also to listen to the relationship when the supervisees are talking from within their own perspective. In this way the supervisor acts like a marital counsellor, in so far as he or she must have the interests of both parties in balance, taking neither the side of supervisee nor of the client against the other.

The supervisor listens to the relationship in a variety of different ways. All approaches involve listening with the 'third ear' to the images, metaphors and Freudian slips that collect around the therapist's description of this particular client. What picture is the unconscious painting of the relationship.

Frank Kevlin talks about listening to the reported therapy as if it were a dream: 'I look at therapy as a dream, the therapist is telling me a dream and

I am doing a dream analysis. The client is the subject being dreamt' (Kevlin 1987).

Attending to the client's transference

The supervisor is also interested in the transference of the client. In Mode Four we will move on to looking at the counter-transference of the therapist, and in many ways it is necessary to move between these two modes and consider the transference and counter-transference together. However, for the time being, we will separate the focus and look only at the client's transference.

Many of the questions used above and paying attention to the images and metaphors will give important clues to the transference that is happening. If, for instance, the therapist said that the relationship was like that of two sparring partners in a boxing ring, the transference would be very different from that of a therapist who answered that their relationship was like a frightened rabbit wanting to cuddle up to its mother.

Learning from the patient

When attending to the process between the client and therapist it is important to recognize that somewhere both parties probably know what is really going on and what is getting in the way of their healthy open meeting. This knowing is most likely unconscious, otherwise the case would not have been brought to supervision. The job then of the supervisor is listening to how the unconscious of the client is informing the therapist about what the client needs and how the therapist is helping or getting in the way. Robert Langs (1978 and 1985) has developed a complex and very detailed system for attending to and then decoding the latent and unconscious communication of the client and then relating this to the interactions of the therapist and how they were unconsciously received by the client.

A simple way to use this approach is to listen to all the reported content of the client, e.g. stories they told, feelings they have about other people, asides and throwaway comments, as all relating to how the client experiences the therapist, especially recent interventions.

Langs (1985: 17 and 20) gives a good example of this process.

> The final session with a 45-year-old woman who was seen in once-weekly psychotherapy for episodes of depression. She begins this last hour as follows.

> *Patient*: One of the boys in the class that I teach at religious school is leaving town. I don't know if I will ever see him again. I wanted to hug him goodbye. My son is leaving for an out-of-town college. I thought of the time my father left us when I was a child. Yesterday, at religious school, I thought of having an affair with the principal.

The patient has largely made use of displacement and symbolization in her allusion to the external danger situation. Rather than alluding directly to the therapist's abandonment ... the patient mentions the loss of a boy in her class, of her son, and of her father in childhood. ... Each involves an aspect of loss and termination and ... each expresses in some disguised form a meaning of the ending of the patient's psychotherapy.

Patrick Casement has written about a very similar approach to Langs in a more easily readable book called *On Learning From the Patient* (1985). Here he writes about 'the patient's unconscious search for the therapeutic experience that is most needed'. He gives ample examples of how the client or patient's unconscious is constantly informing the therapist about its need for *Structure, Responsiveness* and the appropriate *Space*. However, he cautions us to distinguish between patients' growth needs and their wants:

I am here making a distinction between needs that need to be met and wants ... The Therapist should ... try and distinguish between libidinal demands, which need to be frustrated, and growth needs that need to be met.

(Casement 1985: 171–2)

Here is an example illustrating the difference between these wants and growth needs drawn from a psychotherapist one of us supervises:

The therapist was a female worker who looked and acted in a motherly fashion. The client was also a female whose own mother had been very depressed, often not leaving the house for weeks at a time. The client went through periods of *wanting* the therapist to hug and cuddle her and of trying every way possible for the sessions to overrun the ending time. The libidinal demand was for unboundaried symbiotic mothering, whereas the unconscious growth need was for a therapist who would provide the clear boundaries that her own mother was unable to give her. Once this had been realized in the supervision, the therapist's anxiety with this client lessened considerably and she was able to set clear boundaries for the client, in a way that the client was able to accept.

Mode Four: Focusing on the supervisee's counter-transference

In this mode the focus of the supervision is on the internal processes of the supervisee and how these are affecting the therapy they are exploring. It is important to distinguish between four different types of counter-transference:

- Transference feelings of the therapist stirred up by this particular client. This can be either the transferring of past relationship or situation-related feelings on to the relationship with this client; or the projection of part of the therapist on to the client.

- The feelings and thoughts of the therapist that arise out of playing the role transferred on to him or her by the client, e.g. if the client responds to you as if you were her mother, you may find yourself feeling alternatively protective and angry, in the way her mother did.
- The therapist's feelings, thoughts and actions used to *counter* the transference of the client. The client treats you as a mother figure and you find yourself becoming very masculine and businesslike to avoid the mother transference.
- Projected material of the clients, that the therapist has taken in somatically, psychically or mentally.

What all forms of counter-transference have in common is that they involve some form of predominantly unaware reaction to the client by the therapist. It is essential for the therapist to explore all forms of counter-transference in order to have greater space to *respond* rather than *react* to the client. Counter-transference used to be thought of as something that had to be made conscious and removed as it formed a negative barrier. More recently psychotherapists have begun to realize that in the counter-transference can be the clues to understanding the therapy and client better and that working with the counter-transference is a useful therapeutic tool.

It is clear from what we have said above that it would be hard to work with the counter-transference without reference to the client's transference and so Modes Three and Four most often work together. However, there is a difference in focus in whether you are predominantly still trying to understand the client out there, or concentrating more on the supervisee's process.

The simplest way to focus on the counter-transference is for the supervisor just to pose the question 'What is your counter-transference to this client?'; but, as we suggested above, most counter-transference is outside awareness and predominantly unconscious, so this question has only very limited effectiveness.

Another slightly more sophisticated technique is 'Checks for Identity' which we have adapted from 'Co-counselling' (see Heron 1974). In this technique the supervisor takes the supervisee through four stages in order to elicit any transference from a previous person.

Stage 1: The supervisees are encouraged to share their first spontaneous responses to the question: 'Who does this person remind you of?' The supervisor keeps repeating the question until the supervisees discover an answer, which could be a person from their past, a well-known personality or an historical or mythic figure or part of themselves.

Stage 2: The supervisees are then asked what they want to say to the person that they discovered in the first question, particularly what is unfinished in their relationship with that person. This can be done in role play by putting the person on an empty chair or cushion and expressing one's feelings to them.

Stage 3: The supervisees are asked to describe all the ways their client is different from this person.

Stage 4: The supervisees, then in role play, discover what they want to say to their client.

This exercise also fails to get to the more unconscious material, although at times it can lead to surprising discoveries about the most unlikely connections and transferences.

The more unconscious material is often found at the edges of the supervisees' communication. It can be in their images, metaphors or Freudian slips of the tongue; or it may be in their non-verbal communication. The supervisor can elicit this material by getting them to free-associate to images or 'slip' words; or by getting them to repeat and exaggerate a movement or gesture that carries a charge. From these interventions can emerge strong feelings that then need to be related back to the client.

Also when looking at the supervisees' counter-transference it is important to include an exploration of what Frank Kevlin (1987) calls the 'ideological editor'. This is the way the therapist views the client through their own belief-and-value system. This includes conscious prejudice, racism, sexism and other assumptions that colour the way we miss-see, miss-hear or miss-relate to the client.

One way of eliciting this ideological editor is through awareness of the supervisee's use of comparatives or associations. If a supervisee says about a client: 'She is a very obliging client.' The supervisor can ask 'How is she obliging?' 'She is very obliging compared to whom? Tell me how you think clients should oblige you?' Thus the supervisor is seeking to discover the assumptions about how clients should be that are hidden in this comparative term 'very obliging'.

In the terms of Construct theory (Kelly 1955) this supervisee, has a bipolar construct obliging/non-obliging.

Here is another example which shows the eliciting of counter-transference through spontaneous association. It is taken from a supervision session where Robin is supervising a senior manager in a social services department, whom we will call John.

ROBIN: Why are you allowing this staff member to drift and not confronting him?

JOHN: Well I do not want to be a punitive boss.

ROBIN: What would that be like?

JOHN: As you asked that, I got the image of a little boy outside a headmaster's office.

ROBIN: So your unconscious links confronting to being a punitive head teacher. If you were this staff member's head teacher,

> how would you want to punish him and what would you be
> punishing him for?

Having explored this together Robin then encouraged John to try out other
ways of confronting the staff member which were less polluted by the
punitive counter-transference. Thus having started with Mode Four, he
then moved back into Mode Two.

Mode Five: Focusing on the supervisory relationship

In the previous modes the supervisor has been focusing outside him or
herself. In Mode One he or she was focusing on the client and then
increasingly in Modes Two to Four he or she has been focusing on the
supervisee. Increasingly the supervisor has been encouraging the supervisee
to look less for the answers out in the client and to pay more attention to
what is happening inside the supervisee. But the supervisor has so far not
started to look inside him or herself for what is happening. In the final two
modes the supervisor practises what he or she preaches, and attends to the
client's therapy by focusing on how the client's psychodynamics enter and
change the supervisory relationship and then in Mode Six how these
dynamics affect the supervisor. Without the use of Modes Five and Six the
supervisors would lack congruence between what they were asking the
supervisee to do and what they were modelling, i.e. to look inside
themselves.

Harold Searles, an American neo-Freudian, has contributed a great deal
to the understanding of this supervision mode in his discovery and
exploration of the paralleling phenomenon (Searles 1955):

> My experience in hearing numerous therapists present cases before
> groups has caused me to become slow in forming an unfavourable
> opinion of any therapist on the basis of his presentation of a case.
> With convincing frequency, I have seen that a therapist who during
> occasional presentations appears to be lamentably anxious,
> compulsive, confused in his thinking, actually is a basically capable
> colleague who, as it were, is trying unconsciously by his demeanour
> during the presentation, to show us a major problem area in the
> therapy with his patient. The problem area is one which he cannot
> perceive objectively and describe to us effectively in words; rather, he
> is unconsciously identifying with it and is in effect trying to describe it
> by the way of his behaviour during the presentation.

In the mode of paralleling, the processes at work currently in the
relationship between client and therapist are uncovered through how they
are reflected in the relationship between therapist and supervisor. For
example, if I have a client who is very withholding (who had a mother who
was very withholding, who had a mother or father who was very
withholding, etc.), when I present them to my supervisor, I may well do this

in a very withholding way. In effect I become my client and attempt to turn my supervisor into me as therapist. This function, which is rarely done consciously, serves two purposes for the supervisee. One is that it is a form of discharge – I will do to you what has been done to me and you see how you like it; and the second is that it is an attempt to solve the problem through re-enacting it within the here-and-now relationship. The job of the supervisor is to name the process and thereby make it available to conscious exploration and learning, rather than to be submerged in the enactment of the process, by becoming angry with the withholding supervisee, in the same way that the therapist was angry with the withholding client.

The important skill involved in working with paralleling is to be able to notice one's reactions and feed them back to the supervisee in a non-judgemental way, e.g. 'I experience the way you are telling me about this client as quite withholding and I am beginning to feel angry. I wonder if that is how you felt with your client?' The process is quite difficult as we are working with the paradox of the supervisee both wanting to deskill the supervisor and at the same time work through and understand the difficult process in which they are ensnared.

Here is a clear example of paralleling written by our colleague Joan Wilmot.

> I was supervising a social work student on placement to our therapeutic community who was counselling a resident with whom she was having difficulty. He was a man in his forties who had been in the rehabilitation programme in the house for about seven months and was now to move on to the next stage which was finding himself some voluntary work. He was well able to do this but despite the student making many helpful and supportive suggestions, he 'yes buted' everything she said. In her supervision with me, despite her being a very able student, her response to all my interventions was 'yes but'. I took this issue to my supervisor, in order as I thought, to obtain some useful suggestions with which to help the student. However, despite the fact that I was usually very receptive to supervision. I responded to every suggestion my supervisor made with a 'yes but'. He then commented on how resistant I was sounding and how like the resident in question I was being. This insight immediately rang so true that we were both able to enjoy the unconscious paralleling I had been engaged in and I no longer needed to engage in a resistance game with my supervisor. I shared this with my student who no longer needed to resist me but was able to go back to her client and explore his need to resist. His issues around needing to feel his power by resisting could then be worked on separately from his finding voluntary work and he was able to arrange some voluntary work within the week.
>
> (Wilmot and Shohet 1985)

Margery Doehrman has done one of the very few pieces of research on paralleling that exist, in which she studied both the therapy sessions and the supervision on the therapy of twelve different people. In the introduction to her study Mayman writes:

> What is strongly suggested by Dr Doehrman's study, a result that she herself admits took her by surprise, was the fact that powerful parallel processes were present in every patient-therapist-supervisor relationship she studied.
>
> (in Doehrman 1976: 4)

Doehrman discovered that paralleling also went in both directions; not only did the unconscious processes from the therapy relationship get mirrored in the supervision process, but also the unconscious processes in the supervisory relationship could get played out within the therapy process. Mayman concludes by saying:

> I believe parallel processing … is a universal phenomenon in treatment, and that the failure to observe its presence in supervision may signal only a natural resistance on the part of the supervisor and/or therapist against facing the full impact of those forces which they are asking the patient to face in himself.
>
> (ibid.)

The supervisory relationship can also be a forum for trying out new ways of relating. To illustrate this, let us return to the case of Robin's supervision with John, that we used in Mode Four.

> During the session Robin noticed he was irritated with John. He was aware of paralleling, and wondered if this was how John felt about his client. Robin was able to share his irritation in a way that helped John understand his relationship to the client. Also this provided a role model for John of how to share his irritation with the client.

Mode Six: Focusing on supervisors' own counter-transference

In Mode Five we explored how the therapeutic relationship invades and is mirrored in the supervisory relationship. In this final mode we focus on how the therapeutic relationship enters into the internal experience of the supervisor.

Often as supervisors we find that sudden changes 'come over us'. We might suddenly feel very tired, but become very alert again when the supervisee moves on to discuss another client. Images, rationally unrelated to the material, may spontaneously erupt in our consciousness. We may find ourselves sexually excited by our image of the client or shuddering incomprehensibly with fear.

Over the years we have begun to trust these 'eruptions' as being important messages from our unconscious receptors about what is happening both, here and now in the room, and also out there in the therapy. In order to trust these eruptions supervisors must know their own process fairly well. I must know when I am normally tired, bored, fidgety, fearful, sexually aroused, tensing my stomach, etc., in order to ascertain that this eruption is not entirely my own inner process bubbling away, but is a received import.

In this process the unconscious material of the supervisee is being received by the unconscious receptor of the supervisor, but the supervisor is tentatively bringing this material into consciousness for the supervisee to explore.

The supervisor needs to be clear about the counter-transference to the supervisee: 'What are my basic feelings towards this supervisee?' 'Do I generally feel threatened, challenged, critical, bored etc.?' All that has been said above about transference and counter-transference is relevant to the supervisor relating to the supervisee. The main difference is that in supervision you are staying in an adult-to-adult relationship (as far as possible) rather than working *through* the transference. Unless supervisors are relatively clear about their basic feelings to the supervisee, they cannot notice how these feelings are changed by the import of unconscious material from the supervisee and their clients.

In order to use this mode supervisors not only have to be aware of their own processes, but must also be able to attend to their own shifts in sensation, and peripheral half-thoughts and fantasies, while still attending to the supervisee. This may sound a difficult task, but it is also a key skill in being a therapist and it is therefore important that supervisors can model its use to the therapists that they supervise.

Supervisors might use their awareness of their own counter-transference by making statements like:

> While you have been describing your work with X, I have been getting more and more impatient. Having examined this impatience it does not seem to be to do with you, or something from outside our work together, so I wonder if I am picking up your impatience with your client?

> I notice that I keep getting images of wolves with their teeth bared, as you describe your relationship with this client. Does that image resonate with your feelings about the relationship?

> I am getting very sleepy as you go on about this client. Often when that happens to me it seems to indicate that some feeling is being shut off either to do with the therapy or right here in the supervision. Perhaps you can check what you might be holding back from saying?

So far this model explores the inter-play between two relationships: that of the client/therapist and that of the therapist/supervisor; but it ignores the third side of the triangle – namely the fantasy relationship between the client and the supervisor. Supervisors may have all sorts of fantasies about their supervisees' clients, even though they have never met them. The client may also have fantasies about the therapist's supervisor, and we have known some therapy clients to direct a lot of their attention at the unknown supervisor and their fantasies about what their therapist gets up to in their supervision!

These fantasy relationships complete the triangle and like all triangular processes are laden with conflict and complexity. 'Any pairing ousts the third party, and may at an unconscious level, even revive the first rivalrous oedipal threesome' (Mattinson quoted in Dearnley 1985)

Integrating the processes

It is our view that good supervision of in-depth work with clients must involve all six processes, although not necessarily in every session. Therefore part of the training with this model is to help supervisors discover the processes they more commonly use and those with which they are less familiar. We have also found that some supervisors become habituated to using just one process. Always to ask 'What is your counter-transference?' in response to whatever the supervisee shares about their client soon becomes oppressive.

A parallel model to ours is suggested by Pat Hunt (1986) in her article on supervising marriage guidance counsellors. She suggests that supervision styles can be divided into three types:

- Case-centred approach: where the therapist and the supervisor have a discussion on the case 'out there'. This is similar to our Mode One.
- Therapist-centred approach: which focuses on the behaviour, feelings and processes of the therapist. This is similar to our Modes Two and Four.
- Interactive approach: this focuses both on the interaction in the therapy relationship and the interaction in the supervision. This is similar to our Modes Three and Five.

Hunt illustrates the dangers of using one of these approaches exclusively. If all the attention is on the client 'out there', there is a tendency to get into an intellectual discussion 'about' the client. There is also a danger of a large 'fudge-factor' – the supervisee hiding material from the supervisor for fear of judgement.

If the approach is exclusively therapist-centred it can be experienced by the supervisee as intrusive and bordering on therapy. Hunt writes: 'I am not sure how supportive this kind of supervision would feel. I guess quite a lot of learning would occur, but I suspect assessments might be made in terms of the trainee therapist's willingness to open up and talk about himself.' (Hunt 1986: 17).

If the approach is exclusively interactive-centred, there are fewer dangers than in the other two approaches, but a great deal of important information could be ignored in the immersion of the attention in the complexities of the two interlocking relationships.

Thus the trainee supervisor, having learnt skilfully to use each of the main processes, needs help in moving effectively and appropriately from one process to another. To do this, it is important to develop the supervisory skill of timing. The supervisor also needs to be aware of how different modes need to be dominant for different supervisees, and for the same supervisees at different times.

Linking the model to a developmental perspective

It is also important for the supervisor to be aware of the developmental stage and readiness of the individual supervisees to receive different levels of supervision (see previous chapter).

As a general rule new supervisees need to start with most of the supervision focusing on the content of the work with the client and the detail of what happened in the session. As Stoltenberg and Delworth (1987) stress, new supervisees are often over anxious about their own performance and they need to be supported in attending to what actually took place. New supervisees will also need help in seeing the detail of individual sessions within a larger context; how material from one session links to the development over time; how it relates to the clients' outside life and to their personal history. In helping the supervisee develop this overview, it is very important not to lose the uniqueness of the supervisee's relationship with their client, and for the supervisor not to give the impression that what is new, personal and often exciting for the supervisee can easily be put into a recognizable type.

As supervisees develop their ability to attend to what *is*, rather than to premature theorizing and over-concern with their own performance, then it is possible to spend more time profitably on the second focus of looking at their interventions. As stated above, here the danger is that the supervisor habitually tells the supervisees how they could have intervened better. We have found ourselves saying to supervisees statements such as 'What I would have said to this client would have been ...' or 'I would have just kept quiet at that point in the session ...'. Having said such a line we could kick ourselves for not having practised what we preached and wish we had kept quiet in the supervision session!

As the supervisees become more sophisticated, then Modes Three, Four, Five and Six become more central to the supervision. With a competent and experienced practitioner, it is possible to rely on their having attended to the conscious material and having carried out their own balanced and critical evaluation of what they did. In such a case the supervisor needs to listen more to the unconscious levels of both the supervisee and of the reported clients. This necessitates focusing on the paralleling, transference and counter-transference processes being played out within the supervision relationship.

There are some contexts in which the new supervisee will not require this progression of starting in the more content-centred modes, with a later progression into the here-and-now process-centred modes. A psychoanalytic trainee will need their supervisor to use process supervision from

Figure 6.2

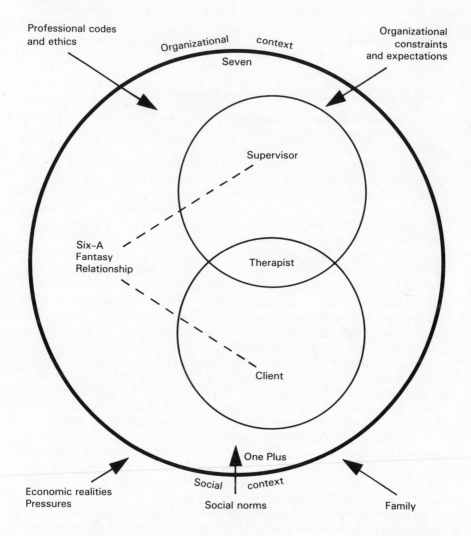

the very beginning and more behavioural counsellors may stay predominantly needing supervision in the content-centred modes.

The developmental stage of the supervisee is only one factor which will cause the experienced supervisor to shift the dominant mode of focus. Other factors that should influence the choice of focus are:

- the nature of the work of the supervisee;
- the style of the supervisee's work;
- the personality of the supervisee;

- the degree of openness and trust that has been established in the supervision relationship;
- the amount of personal exploration the supervisee has done for themselves, e.g. have they been in therapy?

The model within its wider context

Although the six modes of focus are inclusive in so far as they include all the processes within both the therapy and supervisory matrices, the supervisory relationships also exist within a wider context which impinges upon and colours the processes within it. The supervisor can not afford to act as if the client–therapist–supervisor threesome exists on an island. There are professional codes and ethics, organizational requirements and constrictions, as well as relationships with other involved agencies. All of these need to be taken into consideration.

If we were to draw back our viewpoint on the initial model to include the wider perspective our model would be redrawn (Figure 6.2).

In the final section of the book (Chapters 11 and 12) we will explore the wider organizational context in which supervision takes place and how to work with it. Here it is only necessary to note that a fuller model of the supervision process would have to include:

Mode One Plus: the client's wider social context.
Mode Six-A: the fantasy relationship between supervisor and client.
Mode Seven: focusing on the organizational, social and political context in which the work is taking place.

7 Supervisor training and development

This chapter is addressed both to those new or experienced supervisors who want to assess their own learning and development and plan what future training they want for themselves, and to those who are responsible for providing training in supervision. In the second part of this chapter we outline a variety of possible training courses to meet different supervisory training needs.

Assessing your learning needs

There are two attitudes that are often held by new supervisors:

- Now I have been made a supervisor I should know how to do it and should just get on and do the job.
- I do not know anything about supervision and the only way I am going to learn to be a *proper* supervisor is from a full supervision training course.

Both ways of thinking are unhelpful and prevent new supervisors from carefully assessing their own knowledge and abilities and what they need to learn beyond these. Also it prevents them from realizing that the learning to be a competent supervisor can come from a great variety of sources. We believe that a good training course is an essential component of any supervisor's development, but it should be only one of several components. For most supervisees there are a great variety of learning possibilities that can be used in different combinations to feed into each other.

A possible learning programme could look like figure 7.1

This learning cycle can flow in any of the directions and be re-ordered in any way that most suits the learning needs and opportunities of the supervisor. However, if you are to learn systematically you need to start the

Figure 7.1

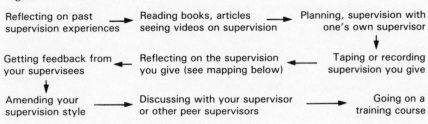

process by carrying out a self-appraisal and learning-needs assessment. We offer the following (Table 7.1) as a possible format for such an assessment, but this is only a blueprint which you can amend and rewrite to fit your circumstances and needs.

Table 7.1   Self-assessment questionnaire for supervisors

	Learning need 1 2 3	Competent 4	Expert 5
Knowledge			
1 Understand the purpose of supervision			
2 Clear about the boundaries of supervision			

3 Understand the following elements:
    managerial
    educative
    supportive			

4 Know the various types of supervision contract			
Supervision management skills			
1 Can explain to supervisees the purpose of supervision			
2 Can negotiate a mutually agreed and clear contract			
3 Can maintain appropriate boundaries			

4 Can set a supervision climate that is:
    empathic
    genuine
    congruent
    trustworthy
    immediate			

5 Can maintain a balance between the managerial, educative and supportive functions			
6 Can end a session on time and appropriately			

Table 7.1 Self-assessment questionnaire for supervisors *(continued)*

	Learning need 1　2　3	Competent 4	Expert 5

Supervision intervention skills

1　Can use the following types of
　intervention (see later in this chapter)
　　prescriptive
　　informative
　　confrontative
　　catalytic
　　cathartic
　　supportive

2　Can give feedback in a way that is (see
　later in this chapter):
　　clear
　　owned
　　balanced
　　specific

3　Can usefully focus on (see Chapter 6):
　　reported content
　　supervisee's interventions
　　supervisee/client relationship
　　supervisee's counter-transference
　　supervision relationship
　　own counter-transference

4　Can describe own way of working

5　Can offer own experience
　appropriately

6　Can develop self-supervision skills in
　supervisees

Traits or qualities

1　Commitment to the role of supervisor

2　Comfortable with the authority inherent
　in the role of supervisor

3　Can encourage, motivate and carry
　appropriate optimism

4　Sensitive to supervisee's needs

5　Sensitive to individual differences due to:
　　gender
　　age
　　ethnic background
　　personality
　　professional training

6　Sense of humour

Commitment to own ongoing development

1　Have ensured own appropriate
　supervision

2　Committed to updating own practitioner
　and supervisory skills and knowledge

3 Recognize my own limits and identify my
   own strengths and weaknesses as
   supervisor
4 Get regular feedback from:
     supervisees
     peers
     own supervisor/seniors

For group supervisors
1 Have knowledge of group dynamics
2 Can use the process of the group to aid
  the supervision process
3 Can handle competitiveness in groups

For senior organizational supervisors
1 Can supervise interprofessional issues
2 Can supervise interorganizational issues
3 Have knowledge of stages in team and
  organizational development
4 Can surface the underlying team or
  organizational culture
5 Can facilitate organizational change
6 Can create a learning culture in which
  supervision flourishes

This form of assessment can be done collaboratively, either by using it as a format for requesting feedback from your supervisees, or by sharing your own self-appraisal with your own supervisor or your work team, and receiving their feedback and appraisal of your work.

Setting up training courses

In the chapter on becoming a supervisor, we argued that it was important that all new supervisors not only obtained supervision on their supervision, but also received some training for the new role of being a supervisor. For some staff it might seem preferable that they receive training before they embark on giving any supervision, so that they have clarity about what they are providing and how they are going to function, before they even start. However, the limitation of this approach is that, like all pre-training, trainees have no direct experience to reflect on and work within their training course, other than their experience of being supervised.

We would recommend that all new supervisors receive a training course sometime within the first year of their functioning as a supervisor. If the new supervisor is in a situation where they do not currently receive good supervision, which can act both as a model and a support for their new role, then the training should precede their embarking on the new role. However, in such cases it is grossly inadequate just to send them on a short supervisor training course and then expect them to function well as a supervisor. The most important part of the development of good supervisors comes not from attending a training course, but from being well supported in planning and reflecting on the supervision that they give. If there is no possibility of new supervisors' receiving this form of support from the person responsible for supervising them, then another possible way for them to find this support is for the training course to set up an on-going peer or led support group for new supervisors to meet and reflect on their supervisory practice.

Another important feature is that all supervisory training should be action based, and not just teaching theory. This means that the course should ideally be a short sandwich course, where the trainees have time in the middle of the course to return to work and carry out some action learning, on the supervision that they either give or receive. Then they will have the opportunity to return to the course and explore their actual experience and how they can handle certain situations differently.

The other important way of ensuring that the course is practical is to make the courses substantially experiential, with much of the time given over to the trainees working together giving, receiving and observing supervision, and then giving structured feedback to each other. On the courses that we run ourselves, much of the time is spent in different triads, with each member having the opportunity to be supervisor, supervisee and observer. Course members report that this is often the most valuable part of the course, with a great deal of learning being experienced in all three roles.

A different way of using triads in training is described by Spice and Spice (1976).

> Working in groups of three, beginning supervisors take turns functioning in three different roles: beginning supervisor, comment-ator, and facilitator. The beginning supervisor presents samples (e.g., audiotape, videotape, case report) of an actual supervision, the commentator reviews the sample and then shares observations and encourages dialogue about the session, and then the facilitator com-ments on the present, here-and-now dialogue between the beginning supervisor and the commentator. Four processes are taught in the triadic model: a) presentation of supervision work, b) art of critical commentary, c) engagement of meaningful self-dialogue, and d) deepening of the here-and-now process.
>
> (Quoted in Borders and Leddick 1987)

Harold Marchant, who has done much to develop supervision training in the areas of youth and community work, writes: 'Supervision involves knowledge, skills and techniques. Above all it involves attitudes and feelings of a supervisor in a relationship with another person, (Marchant in Marken and Payne undated). It is thus important that supervision training includes not only the relevant knowledge, skills and training to equip a competent technical supervisor, but also concentrates on exploring the attitudes and assumptions of the trainees and 'to exploring the concept of empathy and to working out its expression in the supervisory relationship' (Marchant: 40).

All supervisor training must therefore focus on how to build a relationship with a wide range of supervisees, that is built on trust, openness and a sense of mutual exploration. In doing this the trainers need to be very aware of how the course itself is providing a role model and endeavour to provide a setting which is warm, open and trusting, where trainees feel able to explore both their experiences and inadequacies, despite their inevitable fears and vulnerabilities. This is a diffcult task, for as Barbara Dearnley (1985) says:

> I have come to learn that looking in detail at supervisory practice is widely experienced as a very exposing affair, much more so than discussing one's own difficult cases. It is as if the public confirmation that one is sufficiently experienced to supervise leads to persecutory personal expectations that supervisors should say and do no wrong.

Being made a supervisor can decrease the space we give ourselves to be open to learning, for now we can believe that we should have the answers; be the experts; and should certainly not let on that we do not know what we are doing. Guy Claxton described the four beliefs that get in the way of adults' learning as being:

I must be *competent*.
I must be in *control*.
I must be *consistent*.
I must be *comfortable*.

(Claxton 1984)

All these four beliefs can easily be reinforced when a practitioner becomes a supervisor, and doubly reinforced when a supervisor starts training other supervisors!

A training course must set a climate that challenges these attitudes and creates a climate where making mistakes, trying out very different approaches and being vulnerable is valued. To set this climate the trainers have to model not being 'super-competent in-control experts', but experienced supervisors who are still open to and needing to learn and who are also open about their vulnerabilities.

Much of the material that needs to be included in courses is common to all types of trainee supervisors, but there are also different training needs depending on the context in which the trainee supervisor will be functioning. We propose five distinct types of courses. These are:

1 courses for new first-line supervisors;
2 courses for student supervisors;
3 courses in team and group supervision for those who have to supervise teams;
4 advanced supervision courses for those who have to supervise across teams and organizations;
5 psychodynamic supervision courses for those who supervise in-depth counselling or psychotherapy.

We will now look at what each of these courses might include, and we will illustrate this by describing some of the content of our own courses.

1 New first-line supervisors

It is useful to begin the course by ascertaining what experience the course members have of both supervising and being supervised, for both kinds of experience will provide useful material to learn from and will also colour the attitudes and assumptions with which the course members begin their training.

In our early days of teaching supervision we naïvely used to expect course members to be coming on the course already believing that supervision was a good thing and eager to learn how to give it. We were soon disillusioned. We found many staff who had spent years as social workers, doctors, occupational therapists or probation officers, who had never received any formal supervision. There were others whose experience of supervision was very negative. Supervision was a place where they had been made to feel very inadequate by over-critical supervisors. Others had been led to trust their supervisors and share their difficulties and sense of inadequacy, only to find that this had later been used against them by more senior management.

We discovered that it helped course members to be more open if we drew out all the bad experiences and negative attitudes to supervision at a very early stage of the course as this not only stopped them from covertly sabotaging the course, but was also useful learning material. As new supervisors they could explore how not to repeat the negative scenarios that their fellow course members had experienced.

We also learnt from experience to avoid the process whereby we would be very evangelical about supervision and its benefits and the course members would have to carry the negative attitudes. On some courses we introduced a debate where some of the course members would argue for the effectiveness and the benefits of supervision and the others would argue its costs and negative side-effects. Half-way through the debate we would ask them all to switch sides and carry on the heated exchange, but now arguing the opposite case. This ensured that the course was not divided into pro- and anti-supervision factions, and both the costs and benefits of supervision were clearly recognized.

Following this it is important to explore what supervision is. There are many maps and models in Chapter 5 that can be used for this purpose. At this stage trainees should not be over-loaded with too many different theories and maps, but given a clear and simple framework, which can help them identify the boundaries and roles involved in supervision.

This naturally leads on to the issue of contracting for supervision, and the attendant issues of confidentiality, responsibility and appropriate focus. We also find it necessary to explore the setting in which supervision is carried out. Where, when and how does supervision take place? Is it done in a cluttered office with the phone always ringing? Is it done across a desk? What is allowed to interrupt the supervision, or cause its postponement?

We also look at who takes responsibility for arranging the time for the supervision and seeing that it happens – the supervisor or the supervisee? Also how does the supervision start? We often find that the first two or three minutes of a supervision session set the stage and the atmosphere for the rest of the session.

The rest of the time on the first part of our courses is divided between providing new supervisors with maps and models with which to reflect on their supervision and teaching and practising supervisory skills.

The first skill that we teach is the skill of giving good feedback, as this is not only essential to being competent supervisors, but also a skill they will be using throughout the training course as they work with each other.

Supervisory feedback skills

The process of telling another individual how they are experienced is known as feedback. Giving and receiving feedback is fraught with difficulty and anxiety because negative feedback restimulates memories of being rebuked as a child and positive feedback goes against injunctions not to 'have a big head'. Certainly most people give or experience feedback only when something is amiss. The feelings surrounding feedback often lead to its being badly given, so fears of it are often reinforced. There are a few simple rules for giving and receiving feedback that help it to be a useful transaction which can lead to change.

Giving feedback

A mnemonic to help remember how to give good feedback is CORBS: Clear, Owned, Regular, Balanced and Specific.

Clear Try to be clear about what the feedback is that you want to give. Being vague and faltering will increase the anxiety in the receiver and not be understood.

Owned The feedback you give is your own perception and not an ultimate truth. It therefore says as much about you as it does about the person who receives it. It helps the receiver if this is stated or implied in the feedback, e.g. 'I find you ...' rather than 'You are ...'

Regular If the feedback is given regularly it is more likely to be useful. If this does not happen there is a danger that grievances are saved until they are delivered in one large package. Try to give the feedback as close to the event as possible and early enough for the person to do something about it, i.e. do not wait until someone is leaving to tell them how they could have done the job better.

Balance It is good to balance negative and positive feedback and, if you find that the feedback you give to any individual is always either positive or negative, this probably means that your view is distorted in some way. This does not mean that each piece of critical feedback must always be accompanied by something positive, but rather a balance should be created over time.

Specific Generalized feedback is hard to learn from. Phrases like, 'You are irritating' can only lead to hurt and anger. 'It irritates me when you forget to record the telephone messages' gives the receiver some information which he or she can choose to use or ignore.

Receiving feedback

It is not necessary to be completely passive in the process of receiving feedback. It is possible to share the responsibility for the feedback you receive being well given. What is done with the feedback is nearly entirely the responsibility of the receiver.

- If the feedback is not given in the way suggested above you can ask for it to be more clear balanced, owned, regular and/or specific.
- Listen to the feedback all the way through without judging it. Jumping to a defensive response can mean that the feedback is actually misunderstood.
- Try not to explain compulsively why you did something or even explain away the positive feedback. Try and hear others' feedback as *their* experiences of you. Often it is enough just to hear the feedback and say 'Thank you'.
- Ask for feedback you are not given but would like to hear.

Our own emphasis on feedback has been paralleled by that of Freeman (1985). His conclusions are summarized by Hess (1987):

> Freeman (1985) comprehensively outlined a number of important considerations for the supervisor delivering feedback. It should be a) systematic (objective, accurate, consistent and reliable feedback that is less influenced by subjective variables); b) timely (feedback is delivered soon after an important event); c) clearly understood (both positive and negative feedback are based on explicit and specific performance criteria); and d) reciprocal (feedback is provided in two way interactions in which suggestions are made, not as the only way to approach a problem, but as only one of a number of potentially useful alternatives).

Supervisory intervention skills

The other major area of skill learning that needs to be included in any basic supervision training is to review the practitioner facilitation skills of the course members and help them adapt and develop them in an appropriate way for supervision. One useful tool in doing this is the Heron model of six categories of intervention. Heron (1975) developed a way of dividing all possible interventions in any facilitating or enabling process into six categories. They apply equally to one-to-one and group situations. Although they may not be exhaustive, their use is in helping us to become aware of the different interventions we use, those we are comfortable with, those we avoid. Following on from that we can, with practice, begin to widen our choices. The emphasis in definition is on the intended effect of the intervention on the client. There is no implication that any one category is more or less significant and important than any other.

Prescriptive Give advice, be directive, e.g.
You need to write a report on that.
You need to stand up to your father.

Informative Be didactic, instruct, inform, e.g.
You will find similar reports in the filing cabinet in the office.
This is how our card index works.

Confrontative Be challenging, give direct feedback, e.g.
I notice when you talk about the home's supervisor you always smile.

Cathartic Release tension, abreaction, e.g.
What is it you really want to say to your client?

Catalytic Be reflective, encourage self-directed problem-solving, e.g.
Can you say some more about that?
How can you do that?

Supportive Be approving, confirming, validating, e.g.
I can understand how you feel.

These six types of intervention are only of any real value if they are rooted in care and concern for the client or supervisee. They are valueless when used degenerately or perversely. Degenerate interventions happen when the practitioner is using them in an unskilled, compulsive or unsolicited way. They are usually rooted in lack of awareness whereas a perverted intervention is one which is deliberately malicious.

We have widely used this model in helping supervisors look at their own style of intervention. We ask them to appraise themselves in terms of which category they most dominantly use and which category they feel least comfortable using. We then have all trainee supervisors carrying out individual supervisions with a fellow trainee, while a third trainee records the pattern of interventions they use.

This opens up the possibility of the trainees deciding to develop one of their less used intervention skills. Also for many new supervisors it provides an opportunity to consider how their intervention style needs to be different as a supervisor than it was as a practitioner. A non-directive counsellor may find that their previous training and experience have led them dominantly to use catalytic interventions and that as a supervisor they have to incorporate more informative and confrontative interventions.

We have also found that some workers completely switch styles and abandon many of their very useful counselling skills when they move into a managerial or supervisory role. These workers need help in revaluing their own practitioner skills, albeit within a new context and role.

This model can also be used by trainee supervisors in mapping their own supervision style. Some trainees have recorded their supervision sessions and then scored each of the interventions that they have used. Others have used the model for both the supervisee and themselves to reflect back on the session and in particular the supervisors' interventions; then to explore how each party would like the emphasis in intervention style to change.

Mapping supervision

The other main system for mapping supervision that we provide for trainee supervisors is a model that helps them chart the content focus of a session, how it shifts from management issues, to client issues, to areas of supporting the supervisee, and also who is responsible for the shift in focus. This is published elsewhere (Hawkins 1982) and will appear in (Shohet, Hawkins and Wilmot forthcoming).

As mentioned above, the main emphasis of any good supervision course should not be on teaching these skills and models or any others, but on the course members using these skills and maps as a language with which to reflect on the practice supervisions they give on the course, and also the supervision that they give back at work. This is why a central part of the courses is the trainees' returning to work with an action-learning project, using one of the skills or maps as a research tool in order to find out more about their own supervision.

The course needs to reconvene in order to harvest the learning from these action-learning projects, so that course members are learning not only from their own experience, but also from that of their colleagues.

To harvest this learning both discursive case presentations and more action-based methods like group sculpting, role play and brandenburg role-plays can be used (see Chapters 8 and 9). This part of the course can be thought of as an extended group supervision of the course members' supervisory work.

2 Student supervision

There are two types of student supervisors: those who are college based and those who are responsible for supervising students on practice. A training course for both types of student supervisors has to include most, if not all, of the material recommended for new first-line supervisors, but the context and the emphasis of the course need to be slightly different.

First, the college-based student supervisor is working within a different supervision contract, where the emphasis is on the educative and supportive aspects of supervision and where the managerial aspects are being carried by the placement supervisor or manager. Even the placement supervisor will have a greater emphasis on the educative side of supervision.

One of the difficulties for many college-based supervisors is that they are often more at home in a teacher role than a supervisory role. The danger of this is that their supervision may become didactic tutorials, and the supervisees, instead of being enabled to reflect on their own experience, have theoretical references thrown at their 'inadequacies'. 'If only you had read X, then you would not have been so foolish' is the attitude that the student experiences. This is similar to the 'game' that Kadushin (1968) calls: 'If you knew Dostoyevsky like I know Dostoyevsky.' He points out it can be played by either the supervisor or the supervisee (see Chapter 4).

The college-based supervisor needs to provide a climate that goes against the common educational culture of dependency and instead provides a setting in which supervisees are encouraged to be responsible for their own learning and can rely on the support, trust and openness of their supervisor.

At South West London College, where one of us taught and supervised counselling, the students are encouraged to work out their own contracts with both their group and individual supervisor. They are given a blueprint, based on the current staff thinking about supervision. This is similar to the list of supervisor and supervisee responsibilities listed in chapter 3.

Supervisor responsibility

- To ensure a safe enough space for students to lay out practice issues in her own way.
- To help students explore and clarify thinking, feeling and fantasies which underlie their practice.
- To share experience, information and skill appropriately.
- To challenge practice which he adjudges unethical, unwise or incompetent.
- To challenge personal or professional blindspots which he may perceive in individuals or the group.
- To be aware of the organisational contracts which he and the students have with college, employers, clients and supervision group.

Student responsibility

- To herself.
- To identify practice issues with which she needs help and to ask for time in the group to deal with these.

- To become increasingly able to share these issues freely.
- To identify what kind of responses she wants.
- To become more aware of the organizational contracts she is in, in her workplace, in the college, with clients, with the supervision group.
- To be open to others' feedback.
- To monitor tendencies to justify, explain, or defend.
- To develop the ability to discriminate what feedback is useful.

To others (when in group supervision):

- To share with other members all the responsibilities of the supervisor, in such a way that safety and challenge can both be possible in the group.
- To monitor tendencies to advise or compete.

(quoted in Proctor undated)

The other major issue that needs to be focused on in a course for student supervisors is hinted at in the above contract where it says: 'To be aware of the organizational contracts which the supervisor and the students have with college, employers, clients and supervision group.' Most often the student supervisor is part of an extended triangle, with the student having two supervisors (one in the college and one in the placement) and two organizational contexts to work between. We have mentioned in the previous chapter the dynamics that are created in triangular relationships, with the tendency to create splitting, with one supervisor becoming the 'good supervisor' and the other the 'bad supervisor'. Student supervisors need to learn how to negotiate clear contracts not only with their supervisees, but also with their co-supervisor in the placement setting, and also how to carry out three-way assessment and evaluation meetings with the supervisee and the co-supervisor.

3 Course in team and group supervision

Courses need to be arranged in organizations for people such as district occupational therapists, principal care officers in social services, area youth officers or district psychologists who are required to supervise a number of different teams. Such a course would also be useful for experienced team leaders and for training officers who are increasingly finding that they are called upon to provide team consultancy services and not just put on courses.

It would be important that all the people who attended such a course were already trained and experienced supervisors. If not, they should be given some basic supervision training before attending this type of course.

As in the basic course it is useful to start by reviewing the knowledge, skills and abilities of the course members and then looking at what their learning needs are from this particular course. This process is also important as it acts as a model for the course members in how to negotiate a working contract with a group or team.

The course then needs to provide an opportunity to explore the differences between individual and team supervision and to encourage the course members to present the difficulties they have, which are specific to working with teams. Chapters 8 and 9 provide the basis for presenting some of the themes specific to supervising in groups and teams and the course also needs to include teaching on group dynamics, the developmental stages in the formation and growth of a team and some basic theory of team development.

Chapter 9, 'Exploring the dynamics of teams, groups and peer groups', also provides the outline of some of the techniques we teach to team supervisors, both for them to use with the teams they supervise and also to explore their work while they are on the course. Course members can actively involve each other in the dynamics of their supervised teams by using the other group members as a sculpt of a team they would like to explore and then bringing the sculpt to life and have other course members try out various ways of supervising the same enacted group (for a description of sculpting see p. 114).

Another useful strategy for teaching group supervision skills is as follows:

1 Divide the group into two parts – A and B.
2 First the groups meet for a while separately to explore their learning needs.
3 Then group A provides a consultant and a process observer for group B. Group B does the same for group A
4 After a designated length of time the consultants and observers return to their groups to process all three types of experience – that of the consultant, the observer and the members who received consultancy.
5 The exercise can also include structured feedback from the group members to the visiting consultant.

This exercise can continue through several cycles or until every course member has had the opportunity to be in each role.

Where possible the team-supervision course should also be taught as a short sandwich course, so that course members can further explore some of their new perspectives in an action-learning stage, before returning to the course with more monitored experience which they can share with the other course members.

4 Advanced supervision course for those who have to supervise across departments and organizations

Such a course would either be for very senior staff within an organization (e.g. assistant chief probation officers, consultant psychiatrists, etc.) or for those who are either internal or external organizational consultants.

Once again the course members should already have the knowledge, techniques and skills equivalent to those taught on courses 1 and 3. This course would use the material in Chapters 11, 12 and 13 to teach course members how to work with a whole organization or department to help it access its own organizational culture and sub-cultures, and also how to assist it in bringing about organizational change at the levels of *culture* and *ethos, strategy* and *structure*.

At the senior level of any helping profession staff need to receive training, not just in supervision, but in how to give effective leadership to a complex organization that often exists in a hostile and difficult environment. Staff such as chief probation officers, head teachers, consultant psychiatrists, youth directors, etc., need training that teaches them the relationship between management skills, leadership skills and organizational supervision skills.

Recent writers on management have emphasized the importance of directors of commercial organizations being not only first-rate managers, but also having leadership skills (Peters and Waterman 1982; Hickman and Silva 1985; Bennis and Nanus 1985, etc.).

> The problem with many organizations, and especially the ones that are failing, is that they tend to be overmanaged and underled. They may excel in the ability to handle the daily routine, yet never question whether the routine should be done at all. There is a profound difference between management and leadership, and both are important. 'To manage' means 'to bring about, to accomplish, to have charge of or responsibility for, to conduct'. 'Leading' is 'influencing, guiding in direction, course, action, opinion'. The distinction is crucial. *Managers are people who do the things right and leaders are people who do the right thing.*
>
> (Bennis and Nanus 1985)

Leadership skills are becoming increasingly critical for those who are in senior positions in helping organizations. If such organizations are going to continue to learn faster than the rate of environmental change, their leaders need to be conscious of the consumers of their organization's services; the changes in customers' needs and ways of meeting these needs; the staff morale and dynamics; the changes in the local environment; and the changes in national and local political decisions that will affect their organization. There is a great shortage of people who give quality leadership at this level and the training of such people is an urgent priority, not only for the organizations themselves but for the whole country's welfare.

Bennis and Nanus (1985) divide leadership skills into four main types:

- Having a clear vision of where the organization is going.
- Being able to communicate in a way that is both clear and inspirational.

- Being reliable and acting in a way that inspires trust.
- Having a positive self-regard, high self-awareness and a focus on succeeding.

Leaders of helping professions could also do well to start off with Garratt's *Ten necessary characteristics for an effective director (1987)*.

1 I will play down my detailed, specialist function and learn to concentrate on managing the boundaries between my function and the others.
2 From this I will learn how to take an integrated overview of the performance of the total business, and my role in it.
3 I will learn how to delegate, and coach my staff, so that they can do the job for which they are paid.
4 I will give them 'cover' when necessary and will do this for the total organization when we deal with the external world.
5 I will broaden my horizons and role so that I become less political inside the business and more politically aware outside it.
6 I will learn to become competent at exercising both the rights and duties of my directing role.
7 I realize that a balance has to be struck between achieving and nurturing and that it is my job to do this.
8 I realize that our organization is a part of our local and national society so I will try and make decisions which maintain and develop this relationship. We have rights and duties outside our own business to the communities which support us.
9 I will learn to design the future rather than just react to it.
10 I will be seen to have time to think in this organization.

5 Psychodynamic supervision courses for those who supervise in-depth counselling or psychotherapy

This course also has to ensure that its members have already acquired the skills, knowledge and techniques included in the basic supervision course. If not, such teaching would need to be included in this course.

Where this course needs to go further and deeper than the basic course is in understanding the ways of working with the interlocking psychodynamic processes of the therapy relationship and the supervision relationship. We use our own double-matrix model of supervision to teach this area and have developed a series of different experiential exercises to train supervisors in each of the six modes, as well as exercises in how to integrate the modes into their own personal style. (These exercises will be published separately in Shohet, Hawkins and Wilmot forthcoming.)

Conclusion

In this chapter we have emphasized the importance of supervision training that is experiential, practical, involves action-learning and is appropriate to the type of supervision that the course members give. However, supervision courses can never be a substitute for having good supervision oneself.

In teams, organizations or professions that do not have a healthy tradition and practice of supervision, it is unrealistic to try to solve this absence by randomly setting up supervisor-training courses. Supervisor training will always be most effective when it is part of a strategic plan to create an organizational learning culture. How to go about creating the right sort of organization or team climate in which supervision can flourish will be explored at length in Chapters 11 and 12.

PART THREE

Group, team and peer-group supervision

8 Group, team and peer-group supervision

The emphasis so far in this book has been mainly on individual supervision. This is because we see it as the best context in which to address many of the key issues and processes within supervision, before approaching the same issues in the more complex setting of a group.

Group supervision

Advantages

There are several reasons why you might choose to supervise in a group rather than individually. The first of these reasons may be connected to economies of time, money or expertise. Clearly if there is a shortage of people who can supervise, or their time is very limited, supervisors can probably see more supervisees by conducting supervision groups. However, ideally group supervision should come from a positive choice rather than a compromise forced upon the group and supervisor.

The second advantage is that unlike a one-to-one supervision the group provides a supportive atmosphere of peers in which new staff or trainees can share anxieties and realize that others are facing similar issues.

The third advantage is that group supervision gains from the supervisees' receiving reflections, feedback, sharing and inputs from their colleagues as well as the group supervisor. Thus potentially this setting is less dominated by the supervisor, with the concurrent dangers of over-influence and dependency. A group can, when working well, challenge collusions between the supervisor and the supervisee.

A group can also provide a way for the supervisor to test out their emotional or intuitive response to the material presented by checking if other group members have had the same response. This can best be illustrated by referring to the concept of paralleling mentioned in Chapter 6.

We like using the idea of paralleling in groups in particular because the variety of responses of different members can be used to good effect. One of us usually starts group supervision sessions by asking the members to entertain the possibility that we do to others what has been done to us. He introduces the terms introjection and projection, explaining that, if we swallow something without digesting it properly, we may have to vomit it up later. It is usually these cases that are brought to supervision, where some aspect of the client has not been digested. If members of the group can be aware of what they are experiencing, or have been asked to swallow, this can be an extremely useful clue for clarifying what is undigested by the supervisee and client. By using the terms introjection and projection on an easily understood level, he is inviting all the members of the group to trust their here-and-now reactions as part of the supervision work. Here is an example which illustrates the process at work:

> On a supervision course for therapeutic community members, a new young staff member presented a client with whom she had been having difficulty. After an initial enthusiasm and opening up, the client was either missing her session or hardly communicating. As soon as the worker began to present her client, I found myself switching off. I just did not want to be bothered. However, I kept going for about ten minutes asking seemingly appropriate questions until I could stand it no longer. I shared my feelings of uninterest hesitantly – they just did not seem to fit – and group members seemed to be so involved. In fact it turned out that the group was split roughly half and half. One half was very involved and the other half had totally switched off too, but like me was trying to appear involved. The presenter was astonished to see how accurately her feelings for her client of both being very involved and identifying with her, and not wanting to know about her, were being mirrored. The group really began to work well and deeply after that, because permission had been given not only to share apparently negativity, but its relevance was confirmed. This is one way in which the supervisor can check whether his counter-transference is coming from his own psyche or is a useful reaction triggered by the material presented.

The fourth advantage is that a group can also provide a wider range of life experience and thus there is more likelihood of someone in the group's being able to empathize both with the supervisee and the client. Groups are also more likely to have a wider age range, extremely important when you have a young therapist or social worker dealing with clients with mid-life or menopausal issues, or therapists, who have no experience of death, working with elderly clients who are dying. A group provides a greater empathic range not just on the gross level of gender, race or age range, but also of personality types.

Fifth, groups provide more opportunity to use action techniques as part of the supervision. In a group it is possible to re-enact the therapy session with a fellow group member playing the client. This can be developed through the use of sculpting and role-reversal techniques. Below are three in particular, the first described by Gaie Houston (1985). (See also Hawkins 1988.)

> The person presenting the problem, Cecil, sets up the scene he is talking about by first giving a brief outline of what is bothering him. He then goes and stands behind someone he would like to become a central character. He puts his hands on, say, Janet's shoulders, and speaks as if he is the person Janet is to play. For instance: 'I am Rebecca. I am divorced, 50 and Jewish, and lost over 40 members of my family in the holocaust. I suppose I am terribly angry. But all I let out is a sort of dominating sweetness, and I talk and talk through every group session.' Even doing this, Cecil is likely to make more emphatic connection with Rebecca than if he talked about her in the third person. He places other people to play other significant characters, in his group, or in Rebecca's life as he sees fit. Then he casts someone to be himself. 'I am Cecil. Looking at Rebecca I feel rebellious, that I won't let her take over. Then I'm guilty for what she's been through.'
>
> The person who is being enrolled may ask information questions, using the first person. For example, 'Do I see Rebecca as anyone else in my life?' When all are briefed, Cecil watches while the group enacts next week's meeting. They do their best to stay true to what they were instructed, while the new Cecil works to bring a fresh solution. It always prove to be an enlightening experience for the whole group, not just Cecil, often members using the exact words that Rebecca or client uses even though they could have no way of knowing them.

It is possible to follow this form of re-enactment by having several other members trying to handle the same situation, becoming Cecil, while the supervisee (Cecil) becomes the client (Rebecca). This second approach provides an opportunity for the supervisee to discover more about their clients through becoming them and experiencing what it is like to be on the receiving end of different approaches.

It is important that this supervision technique is given plenty of time and there is a chance for each 'therapist' to receive feedback, first from the role-played client, in terms of what was helpful and what was unhelpful or difficult and then from the group, who must likewise give feedback which is owned, balanced and specific. It is too easy to give clever advice and damning criticism from the audience; it is quite another matter to do what you advise on stage (see Argyris 1982).

A third technique that is appropriate for groups is the 'Brandenburg Concerto'. A supervisee presents a client and the rest of the group are enrolled as different parts of the client/worker network in the same way as the enrolling described above. For example, someone could be enrolled as the supervisee's boss who is putting pressure on the supervisee to sort out this difficult client. This is affecting the quality of the supervisee's work, as she does not feel fully present to the client. Someone else can play the boss's boss and explore the pressure he or she is putting on the boss. Someone can play the client's partner who actually is fed up with the client and subtly sabotages any improvement the client makes. The point is that all these (and many more) factors are all present in the one to one but are often not recognized explicitly. The supervisee sees the problem as only to do with the client and does not take into account the system to which the client belongs. What then happens is that there is a short role-play of a session and the rest of the enrolled members listen in role as if they were a fly on the wall. They then feed back their responses in role and the supervisee is astonished to find out that what they say corresponds to the positions the people take in real life. The problem can then be related to the total context, not just the interpersonal or intrapersonal one.

The final advantage of group supervision is that where possible the supervision context should reflect the therapeutic context which is being supervised. Thus, if the supervisees run groups, learning can be gained from the supervision taking place in a group with other group leaders. This provides opportunities to learn from how the supervisor runs the group and also how the dynamics of the presented groups are mirrored in the supervision group (see section on paralleling in Chapter 6).

Disadvantages of group supervision

There are also some disadvantages to supervising in groups. Group supervision is less likely to mirror the dynamic of individual therapy as clearly as would individual supervision.

Also, as soon as you work in a group, you have to contend with group dynamics. These can be a benefit if they are made conscious within the group and used as an adjunct to the supervisees increasing their self-awareness through their part in the group process; but the group process can also be destructive and undermining of the supervisory process if, for example, there is a competitive spirit in the group. The dynamics of the supervisory group can also become a preoccupation. We have both been in supervision groups that have gradually become centrally concerned with their own dynamics almost to the exclusion of any interest in the clients of those present. We will discuss group dynamics more in the next chapter.

The final disadvantage is that there is obviously less time for each person to receive supervision. The individual might therefore only get a turn every three meetings and, if these are held fortnightly, this could, in effect, mean supervision directly for oneself only every six weeks.

Selection of group members

This is a very important part of group life for both members and leaders. Clarity of purpose and needs should be very carefully considered by all concerned, as should range of experience and skills. In terms of size, a supervision group needs to be three people at the very minimum, and no more than seven, otherwise members will have to fight to get enough time and attention.

The group also has to have enough similarity in the types of clients they work with, their general theoretical approach to their work, and their level of accomplishment. However, in a group that is too similar in these three areas the learning and challenge is limited and there is a danger of promoting 'consensus collusion' (Heron 1975).

In the training course that one of us has been running in Bath it has also been important to ensure a geographical mix in the supervision groups, where possible, to limit the possibilities of the group members personally knowing the clients that are presented. This can be a problem in any provincial setting.

Contracting

Once the group has been selected, the group supervisor needs to have the skills to manage the contracting. It is good to ensure clarity of purpose mentioned above – there is often a hidden agenda of getting a bit of therapy on the side, for example, and the group needs to be clear about its policy on this, checking out to see that expectations are realistic. The time factor and the number of clients that can be supervised also needs acknowledging.

Some useful questions for the supervisor to bear in mind are:

- What should be the goals of this group supervision?
- What roles should the group supervisor adopt to permit the realization of these goals?
- What balance between didactic material, case conceptualization and interpersonal process is most productive for trainee learning?
- What is the role of evaluation in this group?

Some of the issues around this are similar to the contracting issues mentioned in Chapter 5, but the issues around confidentiality are more complex. We have found it necessary in some groups to have a ground rule that, if you think you know the client being presented, you declare this and, if necessary, leave the room for the duration of that presentation.

Setting the climate

The next task is to set a safe climate for the supervisees to open up their work to others, a process that always has some fear and anxiety:

- 'Will I be found out?'

- 'Will everyone else find flaws that I am unaware of, not only in my work but who I am as a person?'
- 'Will they think why the hell does he think he can be a therapist with those attitudes or hang-ups?'

The climate must be one that encourages a sharing of vulnerabilities and anxieties without group members being put down or turned into 'the group patient'. It is an easy escape route for group members to avoid their own insecurities by finding a group patient which allows them the chance to return to the much safer role of therapist!

Simple ground rules help to avoid destructive group processes, such as ensuring that all statements are owned and group members speak from their own experience. Avoid good advice: 'If I were you, I would,' and preaching: 'Therapists ought to be warm and accepting', etc. As mentioned above, another useful ground rule is to ensure that feedback from group members is owned, balanced and specific. It is also important the group supervisor ensures that there is a roughly equal amount of sharing between all group members, both in terms of quantity and level of self-disclosure.

Self-disclosure can feel safer if group leaders also share some of their own insecurities, anxieties and times when they do not know, rather than always having to be the one with the answers (see Jourard 1971)

Acknowledging the group dynamic

It is essential that the group leader also ensures that group dynamics do not proceed unacknowledged and finds a way of bringing the dynamics into awareness so that they can be attended to and learnt from, without taking over as the major focus of the group. Awareness of the here-and-now dynamics is an essential part of the learning process but the distinction between a supervision group and a 'T' group, encounter group, or therapy group must be maintained. (For more details see next chapter.)

Structuring the group

For the group supervisor there are a number of choices in how to structure the group session. Which one they choose will depend on the type and size of group as well as their own style and inclination.

One of us starts group supervision sessions, which are part of a psychotherapy training, with a round of each group member stating what issues they have that they would like to bring to the group. This is followed by a negotiation between the competing requests to decide on the order and how much time each person should have.

A variant that can be used with this approach is follow the round by an exploration of whose issue most represents the current 'core concern' of the group. This can be done by asking group members to identify which issue other than their own they would learn most from exploring and then working with the issue that has the most interest. This ensures that the person who is the centre of the work is not just working for him or herself, but has the energy and interest of the group.

Other colleagues divide the group time equally between all those present so that they all know they will get some attention each group. This becomes impractical if the group is too large and/or the time too short.

The group may arrange a schedule where each group member knows in advance that he or she will be the one presenting on a particular day. This makes it possible for some outline notes on the case to be circulated in advance. This moves the session more into a group case study with a greater emphasis on learning from an overview, rather than focusing on current concerns and difficulties. This structure may entail group members' having other supervision for their more immediate supervision needs.

Another option is to trust the process and to wait to see what emerges and where the interest of the group moves. You can also start by checking out what has happened to issues that were explored at the previous meeting.

Supervision style

Group members, unless they are very experienced, will mostly take their lead from the group supervisor and make interventions with a similar style and focus to that of the leader. It is thus very important that supervisors be aware of how they are modelling ways of responding to material that is shared. The supervisor either needs to model or explain that there is a range of ways of listening and responding to what is shared to encourage a multi-layered approach (see Chapter 6).

Team supervision

It is important to recognize that team supervision is different from group supervision. It involves working with a group that has not come together just for the purposes of joint supervision, but have an inter-related work life outside the group. Thus, although many of the approaches to group supervision that we have outlined above are relevant, there are other factors that have to be managed.

There is a difference between teams that share work with the same clients, such as a mental health team in a psychiatric hospital, or the staff of a residential home, and teams which, although they work with similar approaches and in the same geographical area, have separate clients, such as a GP practice or a field social-work team. A simple way of classifying the nature of teams is to use a sports analogy. In football teams all members play the same game, although with different special roles, at the same time and are highly interdependent. In tennis teams the team members play the same game, but do so either individually or in pairs. In athletics teams the members take part in very different sports, at different times, but occasionally work together (relays), train together, combine their scores and support each other's morale.

Casey (1985) warns of the dangers of thinking that all work must be done in teams and provides a model for deciding when teamwork is necessary. Payne and Scott (1982) also provide guidance for considering what sort of supervision is appropriate for which sort of teams.

Supervision in teams that know each other's clients has both advantages and disadvantages, as often in supervision you are attending not to the client 'out there' but to how the client has entered into the intra-psychic life of the supervisee. In a residential home where a staff member, Jane, was exploring her profound irritation with one of the difficult boys called Robert, the other members of the team all piled in with their ways of handling Robert. The supervisor had to work very hard to re-open the space for Jane to explore what it was that Robert triggered in her, who he reminded her of, and to help her generate more options for herself. He created this space by pointing out to the team that the Robert she was struggling with could almost be thought of as a different Robert from the Roberts they were each relating to. This was true on two accounts; first, Robert was a very fragmented and manipulative boy who would present quite differently to each staff member, but also every staff member was differently affected by him, depending on their own personality, history and ways of reacting.

It was crucial in this case that Jane's space was protected or she would have quickly become the staff member seen as the one who couldn't cope with Robert and be covertly elected to carry the helpless aspects of Robert and of the team in working with him. By letting the team flood her with 'good ideas' for dealing with this boy, the supervision would have colluded with intensifying the split within the team and hence in Robert. Certainly after having worked with the feelings of helplessness in Jane and helping her to understand and generate more creative options for herself, it was then possible to return to the team and explore their differing experiences and views of the boy, so that we could gradually put together his fragmentation that had been scattered throughout the team.

When conducting team supervision there are still issues about group selection. Firstly, it is necessary to decide where the boundary of the team is drawn. Do you include assistant staff, clerical staff or trainees? If it is an inter-professional team, issues of inclusion and exclusion are even more highly charged.

Second, good team supervision should alert the team to the danger of the tendency to fill vacancies with 'more people like us'. There is a need for teams to have some degree of homogeneity, but teams also need a balance in personality types, age, gender and skills. Belbin (1981) has carried out a classic study of what range of roles a team needs in order to be effective.

Team supervision also supposes that there is one more entity than the team members needing supervision, as, besides the individuals in the supervision group, the team can be considered as an entity needing supervision itself. We consider the team as an entity to be more than the sum of its parts and to have a personality and intra-psychic life of its own. This is termed by some writers as the team culture or the team dynamic. We will be saying more about this in the next chapter. It is important to note that team supervision is different from other forms of supervision in that it inevitably involves some form of team development.

Steve Fineman (1985) in his study of a social-work department looked at five different teams. One of the teams was significantly more effective in maintaining a high morale and low levels of stress than the other four. One of the key factors in this success was the effective team supervision by the team leader:

> (the) mutual trust established, found links with the team leaders activities in promoting support. Indeed his integrative meetings with staff on professional matters – which he took most seriously and sensitively judging from his and other reports – were probably critical ingredients in helping to set the supportive climate.
>
> (106)

In the following chapter we will illustrate ways of exploring and improving team dynamics and in the organizational section we will discuss how to access and change the culture of both organizations and teams.

Peer supervision

Many professionals on our courses complain that they cannot get good supervision as their immediate line senior has neither the time nor the ability to supervise them. We are often surprised that they have not even considered the possibility of setting up peer supervision for themselves. One of us was in the position of running a therapeutic community and his immediate line manager was the assistant director of a large mental health charity organization who had no direct experience of either therapeutic communities or supervision – a parallel to many of the situations we find with senior practitioners in various professions who are nominally supervised by senior managers with little or no clinical experience. In response to this situation Peter set up a series of peer supervisions. First, he exchanged supervision with his deputy who was more experienced than he in the work with the clients. This worked very well for getting supervision for the work with clients, but did not solve the problems of Peter's receiving supervision on his leadership of the staff team.

Peter's second peer supervision was with the senior trainer within the organization who had spent many years working in a variety of therapeutic communities. Again this worked well for a time, but as both she and he were involved in the senior management meetings of the organization, mutual sharing of their struggles with the management structure became an over-dominant focus.

The third move Peter made was to use the facilities of a professional association, in this case the Association of Therapeutic Communities, to set up a peer-supervision group for senior staff within therapeutic communities. He was surprised to find that many other senior practitioners in voluntary organizations, social services departments and the National Health Service shared the same shortage and need for supervision. This proved a rich and rewarding group with the opportunity to focus on whole-community problems and dynamics. This group went on existing well after Peter and the other original members had left.

This piece of autobiography illustrates how peer supervision can be either individually reciprocal or be in a group of workers with similar needs, approach and level of expertise. It also illustrates how it is possible to look for peer supervisors not only within your immediate workplace but also in similar workplaces within your own organization or with workers from different organizations. We have been involved in helping a number of staff set up their own peer-supervision systems: these include heads of children's homes giving each other reciprocal supervision in one local authority, a group of principal officers meeting regularly for peer supervision in another local authority, and an inter-profession peer-supervision system in a community mental-health team.

One area that has actively encouraged the development of peer supervision has been humanistic psychotherapy. This is partly due to the professional commitment of the profession and bodies like the Association of Humanistic Psychology Practitioners (AHPP) to continuous supervision throughout one's professional career and not only when one is in training. This is backed up by members of AHPP having to reapply for membership every three years, and in their reapplication they have to state what supervision they are currently having.

At present one of us has his own peer-supervision setting for his psychotherapy work which is a peer triad with a consultant psychiatrist/psychotherapist and a clinical psychologist/psychotherapist. At each meeting one of the three members takes his turn at being supervisor. Each of the other two gets forty minutes' supervision. At the end of each person's supervision the supervisee shares with the supervisor what he found helpful and difficult and then the supervisor shares his own reflections of the session. This is followed by the third member, who has been observing, giving feedback, both positive and negative, to the supervisor. This suits the need of those in the triad who receive not only supervision on their psychotherapy but reflections and learning on how they supervise.

Peer supervision clearly has many advantages, but there are also many pitfalls and traps. In the absence of a group leader there is a greater need for a firm and clear structure and it requires greater commitment from the group members.

Gaie Houston (1985) has written about some of the traps or games that we have known peer groups to fall into.

'Measuring cocks' She describes a group where the various members used phrases about their groups such as: 'Mine are so co-operative ...', 'Mine say I have helped them a lot', 'It was such a powerful experience.' She goes on to write:

> An American consultant I know calls this activity measuring cocks. All the statements in it add up to 'Mine's Better Than Yours'. Everyone feels tense, knowing that if one person wins and has the biggest or best, everyone else has lost.
>
> (Houston 1985)

Ain't it awful? In this game the peer group sits around, reinforcing each other's sense of powerlessness. One variant of the game is to spend the time sharing how you must be mad to work for this 'Authority' or 'Hospital'. Another variant is for therapists or counsellors to spend their time showing how clients are hateful, vicious and manipulative beings who resist your best endeavours at every attempt. This can spill over into another game called 'Get the client'.

'We are all so wonderful' Peer-group members can avoid having their anxieties about being criticized or found out by heaping fulsome praise on other peer members as an unacknowledged payment for returning the favour. This becomes a covert form of protection racket and in the long term ensures that that group is too fearful to let new members join or old members leave as this might threaten the unearthing of what is buried. John Heron refers to this as consensus collusion (Heron 1975).

'Who is the best supervisor?' This is a straightforward but often undisclosed or acknowledged competition to fill the void left by not having a group supervisor. It can emerge through group members straining to make the cleverest or most helpful comments, or through distracting peripheral arguments on the efficacy of this or that approach. Peer groups often have no mechanism for dealing with their group dynamics and unfortunately group members who point out the processes that are going on may get caught up in the competition to be the 'supervisor'.

'Hunt the patient' Groups, like families, can identify one member to be the patient and the focus for the inadequate or difficult feelings to which the others do not wish to own. Having an identified patient also allows the other group members to retreat into the safe and known role of therapist and collectively to try to treat the elected patient. A probation officer might be elected to carry all the fear of violence for the peer group. While the other members 'help' this member explore their fears, they also protect themselves from facing the similar fears within themselves.

These games are not the sole prerogative of peer groups, but there is more risk of the group's falling into some of them as there is no outside facilitator whose job (or one of them) is to watch the process. Some of these games will be explored further in the next chapter.

How to form a peer-supervision group

It is clear from the above that peer supervision has many pitfalls, but if properly organized it also has many advantages. In workshops that we have run we are often asked for advice in starting and running peer groups and we generally give the following recommendations:

- Try to form a group that has shared values but a range of approaches. It is important that you can dialogue together within a reasonably shared language and belief system but, if you all have the same training and style of working, the group can become rather collusive and lack a more distant perspective.
- The group needs to be no more than seven people. It must also ensure that it has enough time to meet the needs of all its members. It is no good having a peer-supervision group of seven people, all of whom have a large number of clients for whom they want supervision, unless the group meets regularly for at least two or three hours.
- Be clear about commitment. It is no good the group members' committing themselves because they think they ought to and then failing to meet the commitment. Members must be encouraged to share their resistance to meeting for supervision and, if possible, to share how they might avoid or otherwise sabotage the supervision group. For example, one member may warn the group that he or she is likely to get too busy with more pressing engagements, while another member may say that his pattern is to get bad headaches.
- Make a clear contract. It needs to be clear about frequency and place of meetings, time boundaries, confidentiality, how time will be allocated and how the process is to be managed. You might need to be clear how you will handle one group member's knowing the clients that other members bring for supervision; will the person leave the group while that client is being discussed or will the worker be expected to get supervision on that person elsewhere?
- Be clear about the different expectations. Some members may expect a greater focus on their personal process than others are comfortable with. Some members may expect all their client work to be covered by the group, while others may also have individual supervision elsewhere. Some members may expect a greater amount of advice on what to do next, while others may expect to use role play or other experiential techniques. Try to discover if there are any hidden group agendas. We came across one peer group that consisted of two separate sub-groups that were working out their relationships.
- Be clear about role expectations. Who is going to maintain the time boundaries or deal with any interruptions? Who is going to organize the rooms? Is there going to be one person each time who carries the main

responsibility for facilitating or will this emerge out of the group process?

- Build some time into each meeting (it need only be five or ten minutes) to give feedback on how the supervision process has been for each person. This can include appreciations and any resentments.
- Plan to have a review session every three months when all the members receive feedback on their role in the group, the dynamics of the group are looked at and the contract is renegotiated. Many of the exercises and approaches that are mentioned in the next chapter in exploring the dynamics of teams and groups can be adopted by a peer group in its own review.

There are several other books that give useful hints on establishing peer groups for therapeutic work and, although they have a different focus from peer-supervision groups, they often throw up similar dynamics.

We suggest that those who are interested read Ernst and Goodison (1981); Shohet (1985, Chapter 9).

Organizing a peer-supervision meeting

Many of the suggestions made above about structuring a group supervision also apply to peer-group supervision:

- Set ground rules: e.g. that members give direct, balanced and owned feedback; avoid patronizing advice; time is equally shared.
- Either start each session by discovering who has what needs or have a set rotational system for allocating time.
- Encourage all the members to be clear about what they need from the group in relation to what they are sharing – do they need just to be listened to; given feedback; facilitated in exploring their counter-transference; or helped in exploring where to go next, choosing between various options, etc. It is often useful if you do not know what the person wants to ask – 'What has led you to bring this particular issue today?' or 'What is it you need in relation to this case?'
- Decide about informal time. Often, if you have no social or informal time scheduled, the need to catch up with each other's news, to gossip, and to make personal contact can interrupt the other tasks of the group. Some peer groups schedule a short social time at the beginning and/or end of the supervision group.

Conclusion

Groups clearly have many advantages over individual supervision in the range of possible learning opportunities and different perspectives that they can provide. They also have many potential pitfalls. Those leading supervision groups need to be aware of and work with the group dynamic and this necessitates that they have some training in group leadership and dynamics. Peer groups also need to have a system for attending to their own process so that it stays healthily supporting the task of supervision rather than diverting or sabotaging it.

Ideally the mode of supervision should reflect what is being supervised, so some form of group supervision is essential for those being supervised on their groupwork. Group supervision is also useful in expanding the range of perspectives that one draws upon in reflecting on one's individual work, but we would recommend that, in the case of in-depth individual counselling and psychotherapy, group supervision should be an adjunct to, rather than a replacement for individual supervision. The exception to this is that peer or group supervision can be quite adequate for senior practitioners who have developed not only their own individual competence but also an integrated form of self-supervision (see Chapter 3).

9 Exploring the dynamics of groups, teams and peer groups

In the previous chapter we touched on some of the dynamics that may operate in supervision groups. In this chapter we would like to examine these dynamics a little further and to look at some structures for working with them. For whether your supervision group is led, peer or part of a working team, its effectiveness will depend to a large extent on the ability of its members to be aware of, and process, the group dynamics that prevail. We therefore believe that all those who consider supervising in groups should have some training in this field and we will outline some of the factors that we see occurring most often. This should include understanding the basic stages that groups go through and how to facilitate the group development in the various stages.

Margaret Rioch has written extensively on the interface between supervision and group dynamics. In her *Dialogues for Therapists* (Rioch, Coulter and Weinberger 1976) she charts a complete series of group supervisions (which she terms seminars) with therapists in training. After each seminar she comments on the group dynamics and concludes that 'It is also clear that the group interaction was an important part of the process, sometimes furthering, sometimes interfering, with the learning.'

Most of the theories and our own experience would suggest that groups have to start by dealing with their own boundaries, membership and the group rules and expectations (Schutz (1973) calls this 'inclusion'; Tuckman (1965) 'the stages of Forming and Norming'). This is the contracting stage in group supervision, where issues of confidentiality, commitment to the group, how time will be allocated and what will be focused on and what will be excluded need to be decided and clarified.

Soon after this period of clarifying the basic structure of the supervision group, there is often a period of testing out power and authority within the group. This can take the form of rivalrous competitiveness: 'Who does the best work?', 'Who most cares about their clients?', 'Who has the most difficult cases?', 'Who makes the most penetrating insightful comments?', etc. Or it may take the form of testing out the authority of the supervisor by challenging their approach, trying to show that one can supervise other group members better than they can, or inappropriately applying their recommendations to show that they do not work. This is called the stage of 'Fight/Flight' by Bion (1961); 'Authority' by Schutz and 'Storming' by Tuckman.

It is only when these stages have been successfully handled that the group can settle to its most productive work, with a climate of respect for each individual and without either dependency or rivalry in its relationship to the supervisor.

Rioch's description of the seminars she ran shows how these stages of group development certainly cannot be ignored when supervising in a group. Understanding the theories of group development and having insight into the group dynamics are not enough. The group supervisor must also know how to confront the group process and facilitate positive group behaviour.

In her book Rioch illustrates in detail the importance of confronting the issues of both competition and authority in the supervision group. After a long discussion amongst participants in her seminar she says:

> Could it be that the seminar is skirting around the question of who is the best therapist here? That is no doubt a hot potato, and what is even more hot is the question of who is the worst therapist.

Looking at the issue of competition and group process she writes:

> The issue of competition can contribute to the work of the group if everyone tries to do the best he can. It may also interfere if people become too afraid of being rejected or envied ... In this seminar, as in most groups, there was a strong competitive element. The instructor is trying to point out that this was going on even as people were overtly discussing other issues. Although it was not the primary task of the group to learn about its own processes, it was often desirable to observe what the group was doing, particularly when its processes interfered with the primary task of learning to be useful to clients. The problem in the seminar was to use the students' competition, resistance and transference to the instructor in the service of the task of helping clients.

She also usefully points out that supervisors are also part of the process:

> It may also be helpful to teachers and supervisors to remember that they are subject to the same group pressures that are influencing their students. In other words, teachers and supervisors are competitive,

resistant and reluctant to expose their failures, incompetencies, and insecurities. It is important that they should model for their students, not so much perfection which is impossible, but a willingness to learn from their imperfections.

Receiving authority projections and being comfortable with them are part of both the supervisor's and the helper's role:

> the instructor, who was reasonably well liked on a conscious level by seminar members, readily took on the role of an old witch in the unconscious fantasies of seminar members when they felt, as they sometimes did, like abused children in a fairy tale. Hansel and Gretel were scarcely in any position to be therapeutic to their clients. Neither did they harbour warm feelings toward the old witch whom they shoved into the oven in the happy ending.
>
> (Rioch, Coulter and Weinberger, 1976)

After a discussion in which members of the group hint that it would be better and freer without the leader, one of the members says: 'The real problem is not how nice it would be without her, but how to live with her. And not only with her, but with all the other authorities too.' Rioch sums up some of the ambivalence that we think is very often present in a supervision group, especially of trainees, when she says:

> As mature young people engaged in serious study, the students consciously wanted to use the instructor as a teacher and resource person, not as an adversary to be overthrown or a parent to take care of them. But less consciously, as in all groups, the elements of adolescent rebellion and childish dependency were present and active.

Another pitfall is to engage in therapy (described earlier as 'hunt the patient'). The problem case or member is dealt with perhaps sympathetically but certainly in a way that is subtly putting down. The purpose of this game is that once more the group members can allay these anxieties and inadequacies and move into the more comfortable helping role.

Finally, it is possible to look at the dynamics of supervision presentation in terms of how you might consider a dream. When Robin runs dream groups, he does not pay attention only to the actual dream, but to when in the group life it is told and how it is told. For example, if someone tells him a dream in which the dreamer is struggling to get somewhere, and is angry that no one is helping him, he holds the hypothesis that the dreamer could be feeling this way in the group as well as in the dream. The way the dream is told can also give clues. A dream in which the person could make no headway was reflected in the group as the group struggled for different ways of working with the dream and were blocked with 'yes buts'. Similarly a supervision case can be a statement to the group and a reflection of how the supervisee feels in the group expressed through the client.

An example of this occurred with a trainee who was having a very hard time staying on one of our courses. She presented a client who was near to despair and was wondering if it was too late for her to work with this client. The group offered helpful suggestions but nothing seemed to help until the supervisor suggested that maybe she was afraid that things had got too bad on the course, and that it was too late for her, the counsellor, to put things right. This was a tremendous relief, as she realized how she was trying to communicate her despair to group members via the client.

Another time there was extreme tension and lack of progress in a supervision group and someone volunteered to present a case. It seemed a trifle masochistic as the group was not in a supportive place. We suggested that she make sure that she did want to present. Despite her reassuring us that the group tension did not bother her, we decided to pay attention to group process rather than just blindly work with the material presented. It turned out that she was working in an establishment where she felt other staff members were using her to do their work. The parallels with what was happening in the group became obvious. It also transpired that she was the one in her family who always tried to sort things out, so this issue of working for others was operating on three levels – family, work and here and now in the group. By commenting on the group process we were able to make sure she did not get stranded in the here and now and were able to facilitate the group as well as the individual.

Facilitating group or team reviews

In our roles as consultant and supervisors we have been called in to help groups, teams or peer groups explore their dynamics and to facilitate them in finding better ways of functioning. This has ranged from a simple one-off meeting to an in-depth three-day team-development session. Whatever the length and whether it is a team, group or peer group, some of the issues we would explore and how we would explore them would be the same.

Contracting We would begin by clearly contracting with the group members as to what they want from us as consultant. This would entail asking intentionally naïve questions, such as:

- What is the purpose of your meetings?
- What do you expect from one another?
- Why have you called me in as a consultant? and why now?
- How would you know if this consultancy had been successful for you? What specifically would be happening differently?

Clear contracting is not only important for the success of the consultancy but it also models the way members of the team or group can contract among themselves, both about how they meet generally, but also how each person can be pro-active in negotiating with the group his or her supervision needs.

Giving feedback   Before looking at what the group can become, it is necessary to start by finding out more about what it already is. One way to do this is for each person to receive feedback from all the other group members on what they have appreciated and found difficult about his or her contribution to the group.

Then each person can say what they have most appreciated and found most difficult about the group as a whole. This provides the beginnings of three lists: what the group values and needs to build on; and what it wants to change; and what is missing and needs to be introduced.

Estrangement exercise   This provides another means of getting at the issues in the team or group that need to be addressed. In this exercise each member takes on the role of a person, totally different from the role player, who might attend an international conference on supervision. This person could be from a foreign country, be a different gender, be a member of the press, etc. It is important to choose somebody who will see things very differently from you, but whose perspective you are able to take up.

When the group members have taken up their roles and given themselves names, they are asked to close their eyes and relax. They are then led through a fantasy of arriving at the international conference, meeting people, hearing talks, etc. Then they find they are going on a visit to a supervision group to see how it operates. The group they visit happens to be the group they belong to in their everyday personas. In the fantasy they are directed to attend to what they notice when they first arrive, how they are received and by whom, how the group gets under way, who initiates, what the starting rituals are, what other roles are taken up, who is most verbal, who least verbal, what is the non-verbal behaviour and what is it indicating, what do they feel as they watch the group proceed, how does it end and what happens after the ending.

Still in the fantasy they say goodbye to the group and return to the conference where there is a message awaiting them, asking them to write to the group they have just visited and give them feedback. This is requested to be in the form of:

- What did you think was most positive about the group that needed to be built on?
- What do you think was most problematic that needs to be changed?
- What is one new thing that you think the group should introduce?

Still in role, people come out of the fantasy journey and actually write their letter from their assumed role to their own group. Having signed off and de-roled, they then read either their own or each others' letters to the group and the issues are collected under the three different headings.

This can provide an agenda for exploring changes in how the group functions, leading to a recontracting stage. But it is also possible to go deeper in exploring the unconscious dynamics.

Exploring the group dynamics   Some useful statements that can be used in exploring the deeper dynamics of groups are:

- The unwritten rules of this group are ...
- What I find it hard to admit about my work is ...
- What I think we avoid talking about here is ...
- What I hold back on saying about other people here is ...
- The hidden agendas that this group carries are ...

Sculpting the group   This is an approach taken from sociodrama but which we have adapted and developed for exploring the underlying dynamics of teams and groups.

Stage 1 The group is asked to find objects or symbols that represent what is at the heart or core of the group. These are placed in the centre of the room.

Stage 2 Without discussing it, the group members are asked to stand up and move around until they can find a place that symbolically represents where they are in the group, i.e. how far are they from the centre? who are they close to and who are they distant from? Then they are asked to take up a statuesque pose that typifies how they are in the group. This often takes several minutes as each person's move is affected by the moves of the others.

Stage 3 Each person is invited to make a statement beginning: 'In this position in the group I feel ...'

Stage 4 All the members are given the opportunity to explore how they would like to move to a different position in the group and what such a move would entail for them and from others. For example, one person who has sculpted himself on the outside of the group might say that he would ideally like to be right in the middle of the group. Having verbalized this desire, he would be invited to find his own way of moving into the centre and seeing what that shift felt like for him and for the others in the middle.

Stage 5 The group is asked to reframe the group by being asked – If this group were a family what sort of family would it be? Who would be in what role? Who would be the identified patient? etc. Or if this group were a television programme which programme would it be? Again who would be in what role and what would be the transactions?

It is also possible for the groups to try out their own frames. There are countless possibilities – meals, animals, countries, modes of transport, myths, Shakespearean plays etc.

Stage 6 Then a chair is introduced as the 'Creative consultant's chair'. Each person is invited to go and sit in it and to make a statement: 'If I were the creative consultant to this group I would ...' This gives the opportunity for each person to leave their own role-bound perspective and to see the whole system and to make a comment from outside.

Exploring the wider context in which the group exists   All teams and groups exist within a wider context which they are both affected by and affecting. Thus a social work team exists in the context of the clients it work with, the whole organization of which it is a part, the other agencies it works alongside, the ratepayers and the council that controls its activities.

A peer-supervision group of psychotherapists may have a different context. The sorts of people they affect and are affected by may include their clients, their families and friends, their own therapists and any individual supervisors they also see.

This wider system can also be sculpted through what we call an enacted-role set.

Stage 1   The group or team brainstorms all the significant roles that are affected by and/or affect the group. It then selects the most important roles and relationships that need to be explored.

Stage 2   One person takes on the role of each of these aspects of the wider system, e.g. one person represents all the clients, one person the partners of the group members.

Stage 3   The group is symbolically placed in the middle of the room and the various roles place and sculpt themselves in relation to the group.

Stage 4   Each role makes three statements:
What I offer this group is ...
What I expect from this group is ...
What I see happening in this group is ...

Stage 5   It is then possible to explore dramatically a dialogue between the group and the people and roles that it relates to.

Having completed this exercise the group can look at how it would like to change the relationships with those with whom it inter-relates. Here is an example:

A community-work team were exploring how they could improve their team's functioning. They did this in a two-day team-development workshop. The first day they worked on their internal dynamics, support and supervision arrangements and had given each other a lot of feedback. On the second day they wanted to explore how they could change their relationship with the wider network. They began by brainstorming to establish who were the significant others in the wider network who had a stake in how they operated. From this list they choose to explore the relationship to the following 'stakeholders'.

the senior management team
the director of the community-leisure department to whom they
were responsible
the community-leisure committee
the ratepayer
the personnel department of the council

the social-work department
the education department

All of these roles were taken on by the team members who sculpted themselves in a position in relation to the other stakeholders and to a chair that represented their community-work team. Each person in role then used the three statements:

What I offer this team is ...
What I expect from this team is ...
What I see happening in this team is ...

There was much laughter, amusement and surprise, as they found they were able to say many challenging things about their own team, when speaking from the role of the other stakeholders.

They were also able to explore dramatically the relationship with some of these stakeholders by creating a dialogue in which one team member would speak for the team and another would respond in the role, for example, of the education department.

Conclusion

Whether you work in a team, or have supervision in a group or peer group, it is important that there is regular attention paid to the dynamics that are operating within the process. In supervision groups, as in any other group, there are task needs (to attend to the improvement of the work done with clients by the group members); individual needs (for support, reassurance, approval, acceptance, etc.); and group maintenance needs (to deal with the issues of competitiveness, rivalry, authority, inclusion/exclusion, sub-grouping, etc.).

Where there are good group or team supervisions, they will try to see that all three types of needs are attended to and are in some degree of alignment with each other. However, the team leader is not only someone who can attend to the dynamics, but also part of the dynamics that are operating. Also the team or group supervisors are inevitably limited in the amount they can be aware of in such a complex system. Thus there is a necessity to build some structures whereby the whole group is able to share in the responsibility for focusing not only on the task needs, but also on the individual and group maintenance needs.

Some structures can become a regular part of group-supervision meetings, such as spending ten minutes at the end of each group, with each group member saying 'What I have most appreciated about this session has been ... What I have found most difficult about this session has been ...' Other structures may take place at greater intervals, such as an agreement to have a review of how the group is functioning every three months, with structured feedback to the group facilitator and to each member.

Teams that work regularly and intensively together need also to take regular time away from the pressures of the front-line work to stand back and look at how they are individually and collectively functioning, and how they relate to the wider system in which they operate. This may take the form of an away-day, or a team-development workshop, or sessions with an outside consultant, or may be part of a larger organizational change and development programme. The last of these three we will be exploring in Chapter 12.

Whichever way a team or group decides to follow in managing their own dynamic, it is good to remember that the time to start focusing on what is happening in the dynamics is when things are going well and not to wait until the group or team is in a crisis, for then the levels of conflict, hurt and fear make it much more difficult to see what is happening and to take the risk of making changes. However, for some teams it is only when they hit a crisis that they create the motivation to face what is happening and sometimes 'crises create the heat in which new learning can be forged' (Hawkins 1986).

PART FOUR

An organizational approach

10 Supervising networks

In the previous chapter we have advocated the need for supervision at all levels – the individual, the team, the department and the organization. We also recommend that each level is supervised as a whole entity, e.g. the department is supervised with regard to how it functions as a department. This supervision is essential if each level, whether it be in a social-work department, health service or school, is going to provide a measure of containment, holding and understanding for what happens within it.

We sometimes describe the containment process in a way that one organization called 'the bucket theory'. All helping organizations are, by their very nature, importing distress, disturbance, fragmentation and need. This is usually met by individual workers, who, if they are empathically relating to the client's distress, will experience parallel distress and sometimes disturbance and fragmentation within themselves. How much of this they will be able to contain and work through will depend on the size of their emotional container (or bucket), will relate to their personality, their emotional maturity and professional development, the amount of pressure and stress they are currently under at work and at home and, most important, the quality and regularity of the supervision they receive.

What is not contained at this level will lead to decreased functioning in the worker and can also lead to fragmentation in the team. This comes about as workers who are stressed most often act out this stress on their colleagues. They can get irritable with the secretary, angry with their boss and non-co-operative with their colleagues. Fights can develop about who is responsible for what, and arguments over duty rotas. Team meetings begin to start later and later.

In the chapter, 'Group, team and peer-group supervision', we talked about the need for the team to take stock of how they were functioning, individually and as a whole unit, and good team supervision increases the ability of the team to contain pressure, stress and disturbance.

What the team does not contain can once again spill further out into the department or organization. Communication channels are often the first to suffer, with projections increasing both from the team on to management and other teams, but also on to the team from other parts of the organization.

The team can become either the identified patient or the scapegoat for the organization – their problem child (see the section on the pathologizing culture in Chapter 11). Being either the identified patient or the scapegoat means that the team has not only its own problems but can have the disturbance from elsewhere in the organization projected onto it.

The organization needs good regular supervision and time when it stands back and reflects on its own health and functioning. Particularly in times of cuts in resources this is essential, but often ignored. The result is that consultant psychiatrists or directors of services stop working co-operatively and start to fight each other for diminishing resources and basic-grade workers retreat back into the enclaves of their own teams.

Some of this organizational supervision needs to be done by the leader within the organization. As Mao Tse-tung said, the job of a leader is to give back to the people clearly what the people give to the leader confusedly. However, few heads of caring organizations receive good training in the skills required for supervisory overview and leadership of the organizational processes. Being a leader requires different and additional skills from being a good manager.

Also no matter how good the leadership and 'helicopter skills' of consultant psychiatrists, directors of social services or heads of schools, they will always be part of the organizational system they are also trying to support and supervise. This will mean they will also be part of the problems of that system, and unconsciously trapped within the perspective of their particular organizational culture.

What the organization does not contain, process and understand, can then spill over the boundaries of the whole organization and get played out between professions and organizations. This is not only enormously costly to all the helping professions, but very hard to supervise. Even so, some form of outside consultancy supervision is nearly always necessary.

Here are three case studies of a client's process being enacted between a variety of professional agencies. We wish to explore how supervision both within and between these agencies could address the complex issues involved; how it could help the staff to work together in the interests of the client, rather than enact the client's process through interprofessional rivalries.

To avoid breaching confidence, significant details of the cases have been changed and material from more than one case has been combined. However, the cases are in essence both true and typical of inter-organizational working as we experience it, working across a large number of different agencies.

Case A

The first is a case which illustrates the way clients involve a whole network of helping professionals, often with different expectations. We include it in order to illustrate how in many situations clients are involved with a numbr of helping professionals, each of whom has a personal investment in and perspective of the client. In such cases the supervisor cannot afford to focus only on the worker and his or her relationship with the client, but must also focus outwards on the network of professionals and how they are enacting the various aspects of the client.

The client, whom we will call James, had spent several years in a special hospital for the criminally insane for burning down supermarkets. He had been sent to a halfway-house therapeutic community, in order to be gradually rehabilitated back into the community. Any re-offence would mean his immediate recall to the special hospital.

The counsellor in the therapeutic community has not only to relate to the expressed needs of the client (James) but also to cope with the pressures and demands of the personal and professional network with which James is involved.

The hospital is anxious that the therapeutic community ensures James has no opportunity to re-offend. The local probation officer, who is greatly overworked, whose team is understaffed and who is thus under a great deal of pressure, wants the community to keep James 'off her back'. James has taken to phoning her every time he is at all upset or lonely in the community – a bit like the way a new boy at boarding school might phone his mother.

James's parents want the community to help James to return to their very religious and Victorian values, the deviation from which they see as the start of his problems. They insist that the local priest calls regularly.

The local authority, which is paying the fees for James to be at the community, want to know when he will be starting work and thus reducing their financial burden.

James himself is ambivalent. Part of him wants to open up and explore himself in the groups and counselling; but part of him wants the staff by magic to remove his seething anger or to give him the early parenting that he never received. He presents as very cool and together, with no problems at all. All his anxieties and fears he feeds into the other professionals outside the community. The counsellor cannot understand why the others are all getting so worried and needs to be helped by their supervisor to see how James's process is being acted out on a network level. The supervisor also had the responsibility to work with the network to help them understand not only how they are part of the therapeutic team, but that their behaviour is also likely to be a symptom of James's process.

In any situation where there is more than one helping professional involved, it is important that the network meet and decide both who is the key worker, and whose task it is to manage and supervise the helping network (this ideally should be the supervisor of the key worker).

Case B

A London girl in her early twenties is seeing a counsellor who is based at a
GP practice. Her father had died the previous year and the mother, who has
always suffered from mild depression, was unable to give her much support.
The girl is unable to cope at college, and the GP has given her low-grade
anti-depressants and sent her on to the resident female counsellor. The
counsellor works slowly and steadily with the client seeing her fortnightly
for hourly sessions. The client is quite defensive and only slowly opens up.
If there is a very emotional session, the client tends to miss the following
appointment.

After a year's work the client is still having difficulty and over-eating,
although she has been back at college for six months. She develops low-
back pain which again necessitates her missing college. The counsellor
mentions an osteopath that she herself goes to see. The client goes to the
osteopath and at first is delighted. The treatment seems to ease the pain and
makes her feel a lot better about herself. Then suddenly a session with the
male osteopath inadvertently awakens feelings about sexual interference by
a man (unnamed) and, as a consequence, she stops seeing both the
osteopath and the counsellor.

The client gets worse and the GP, who is now anxious, refers her to the
local psychiatric outpatients' department, where a young registrar decides
to take her on for psychotherapy, without any prior consultation with the
counsellor.

Clearly the client's process is being played out, not within a contained
therapeutic situation, but through multiple transference on to four different
professionals. The professionals are not only failing to work together to
bring about some integration of the various fragments of the client's
process, but are also enacting some of the typical interprofessional rivalries
endemic within and between each of their roles.

Any situation, where splitting and multiple transference are ensuring that
no one helper can work with the whole process, requires the difficult
supervision process of a case conference. In this case the case conference
needs to involve the GP counsellor, osteopath and psychiatric registrar and
perhaps even the tutor from the college. To make this happen would require
overcoming several major hurdles:

- The client is working unconsciously to keep the various professionals
  apart.
- It is unlikely that all these busy professionals would be willing to give the
  time for this case conference concerning a client who is not in a major
  crisis (yet).
- The different professional trainings militate against interprofessional
  work. Orthodox and complementary medical practitioners mostly
  distrust each other and avoid working together. Some medical training
  teaches doctors to treat other staff as 'ancillary paramedics'.
- There would be issues of who convenes such a meeting and who would

provide the supervisory overview. If no one provides this overview, there would be a distinct danger that the case conference would just enact the client's process, rather than come to a better understanding and a new way of working with it.

Clearly supervision could have helped this situation. The place where it could have created the most change would have been in the supervision of the psychiatric registrar who needed different supervision from what he was receiving. He attended a weekly supervision group with the consultant psychiatrist where he would present a case only once every six weeks, and this would be focused on in terms of the one-to-one relationship. In this case such supervision would tend to ignore the wider social network where most of this client's process was being enacted.

It is probably the psychiatric consultant who could best call a case conference and, instead of the psychiatric service's taking over the therapeutic work, its skills and resources could be used to relocate and help support the therapeutic work back in the community, with the front-line workers.

The GP team needed supervision to explore why the GPs referred patients to the psychiatric services often out of a somewhat panic reaction to a deterioration in a client and before first exploring the case with their own counsellors and health visitors who were also involved. Often the GPs referred to the counsellor clients who were burdening them with their neuroses, but, if the same client later turned up at surgery in a way that was disturbed or disturbing, the GPs would tend to refer to the psychiatric hospital without first checking what was happening in the counselling. This would happen despite the fact that the counsellor was better trained therapeutically than the junior registrars who would normally see clients at the hospital.

Supervision could also increase the amount that the other involved professionals learnt from this experience. The counsellor could have been better supervised in exploring her unconscious motivation in referring the client to her own male osteopath.

The osteopath also needed supervision that would help him be alert to signals from women clients who had a history of sexual abuse and also learn how to work with such clients in an appropriate, sensitive and therapeutic way and when to refer on to a female colleague.

Case C

A sixth-form student, at a boarding school in the Midlands, came to the psychiatric hospital, near her home in the Home Counties. She had been anorexic for two years. She had a sister of 15 and two half-brothers who were twins aged 3. Her own father had left home when she was 12 and she still idolized her lost father.

She initially confided to her school mistress that she had been interfered with sexually by two men – both unknown. This was shared with the hospital. The young woman was first seen by the male consultant, but then referred by him to a female nurse/therapist who was part of his team, and whom he supervised. There was soon evidence of splitting and multiple transference with the teacher becoming the 'bad person' and the therapist the 'good and helpful' adult. This splitting later spread to the two involved organizations. The girl had gone to hospital at Christmas as an in-patient, rather than go home. She told the school that she wished to do so again at Easter and they told her that, if she did, she would not be allowed back at the school. Despite this she was admitted to hospital and was treated twice weekly by psychodynamic psychotherapy from the same nurse-therapist.

During the next three months, without any behavioural techniques being used, she put on over a stone in weight. As she did so, she became progressively more distressed and unhappy and required medical treatment with an anti-depressant to help her sleep and to help her feel less distressed.

It came to light in the therapy that the girl had been sexually abused by the stepfather. It was thought that this abuse was only mild, but the precaution was taken of informing the family GP in case the younger twins were at risk. The GP was confident that the twins were well and that there was no sign of abuse, physical or sexual.

It was thought that the abuse by the stepfather was not serious enough to warrant further action and the breaking of the patient's confidentiality. As a precaution the supervisor contacted the Medical Defence Union and asked under what circumstances confidentiality could be broken and was informed that, if a serious crime had been committed by someone, then it was appropriate to break confidentiality. The local health-authority regulations suggested that a wide variety of people should be informed at the slightest suggestion of a child being at risk of abuse. This includes the chief medical officer, social services, the police and the general practitioners involved.

The young woman then informed the psychotherapist that the abuse had been severe and had involved full sexual intercourse for about two years. The therapist and supervisor later discovered that she had informed the therapist the day before her sister was due to return home, i.e. that she was unconsciously protecting her sister. When asked about her sister she at first said that her sister was not at risk, but then explained that the sister was not at risk as long as she herself was at home to protect her.

After receiving the information, the supervisor arranged to contact the mother and stepfather to confront them with the information. He felt that he was now responsible to protect the at-risk sister, but was still in a dilemma about whether or not to involve social services. His previous experience of involving social services and the police in such situations had not been good, for it had led to increased distress within the family, but rarely to any resolution of the family situation, or acceptance of responsibility by either the perpetrator or the mother.

The supervisor and therapist were also anxious about breaking confidentiality. The client had been informed that all information shared in the therapy was confidential, but that on occasions the psychotherapist would need to discuss the case with her supervisor. The therapist and supervisor were both beginning to feel distressed, anxious and angry themselves.

The supervisor rang the relevant social-service team leader to discuss the situation in theory without mentioning names but, after a short discussion, made a unilateral decision to make an official warning of possible child abuse.

The supervisor explored the situation in his own supervision. What had made him change his mind, and why was he carrying all the responsibility for the patient, the patient's sister and the therapist? He explored how he felt filled with feeling not only totally responsible for the whole system, but also helpless and vulnerable. Of how he identified both with the patient (he himself had experienced a lot of distress as a boy) and with the perpetrator (being male, a father and someone whose job gave him power over people).

The case was extremely intrusive and produced distress in the supervisor and therapist, even when they were not at work. They half shared their feelings in an interdisciplinary staff meeting, but this led them to feel unsupported and as if they were receiving all the disowned anger and hostility of the other staff.

Through supervision the psychiatrist was helped gradually to express the great mixture of feelings that he was carrying in relation to this case. Only when these had been supportively listened to by the supervisor, could the psychiatrist be challenged about why he was taking on board feelings and responsibilities that did not belong to him. The psychiatrist became aware of how he tended to use omnipotence as a defence and how this was not only a personal trait, but also something that was part of the culture of medical training.

The psychiatrist also began to explore his failure to challenge the therapist to confront the situation with the patient. Instead he had enacted once again the conflict's being taken one stage further away from the family where it belongs and being carried by others. First the abused daughter was forced to take the conflict which belonged to her stepfather. Then the teacher and therapist start to carry the conflict for the girl. Then the psychiatrist takes away the responsibility. The psychiatrist's supervisor could have been next in line, had they not recognized the process as it was happening and started to put the responsibility firmly back where it belonged.

The nurse therapist needed support from the psychiatrist in pointing out to the patient how she was unconsciously worried about her sister's being abused, feeling responsible, but understandably not wanting to accuse her stepfather, but also secretly wanting to punish him, not only for the abuse, but for being the intruder in the family position that rightfully belonged to her real father.

By the therapist's allowing the psychiatrist to take over, she was leaving the process to become once more one between a young girl and an older man in authority, thus replicating the role of opting out and turning a blind eye that the mother had played.

The patient and the therapist needed then to be active participants in deciding how to manage the dilemma. Even if the patient opted out from any responsibility of confronting the situation, she needed to be constantly informed of what the therapist and the psychiatrist were doing.

Then instead of the family's being handed over to either the social services or the police to deal with, the social services should have been brought in to meet with the girl and the therapist (with the psychiatrist as supervisor to the case conference) to work as a team on how to tackle the situation. If it became clear that the stepfather had carried out a criminal act, then the police would have to be added to this therapeutic team.

Throughout this process, it is important that the distress and vulnerability do not get separated from those carrying the responsibility and potency. The two must be kept together in order to avoid splitting and to make contained therapeutic work possible.

The Butler-Sloss report (1988) that followed the enquiry into how cases of suspected sexual abuse were handled in Cleveland recommended much greater co-operation between the health service, social services, police and GPs. One of the difficulties in putting this important and valid recommendation into practice is that of providing good supervision in these multi-disciplinary settings. As I have illustrated in the two cases above, it is not enough for there to be good supervision within the respective disciplines; there must also be supervision of the whole therapeutic network.

One simple model which can help understand such cases, and how they can get played out between agencies is the triangle of persecutor, victim and rescuer. In this model not only do each of the roles get caught within the system, but the roles can suddenly shift around. Let us illustrate this from the Cleveland situation (Butler-Sloss 1988, see also Campbell 1988).

The situation began with two doctors believing they had diagnosed sexual abuse in over a hundred cases. They recommended to the social services that these children be taken into care. At this stage the triangle appears as Figure 10.1.

There soon develops a massive outcry from the parents and disbelief by the media that sexual abuse can be so widespread. The local MP and a number of local and national papers start a crusade to rescue the victimized families (Figure 10.2).

But as in many such triangles the rescuers turn on the persecutors, they call for their dismissal and paint them as villains who are evil, rather than as dedicated professionals trying to do their jobs. The female doctor involved is portrayed by some popular newspapers as almost a witch, intent on breaking up innocent families. The triangle becomes as in Figure 10.3.

Like all such processes, this could have continued for a long time. The only way to stop the process is for one of the elected rescuers not to turn to persecuting the previous persecutors, but to understand the process as a

Figure 10.1

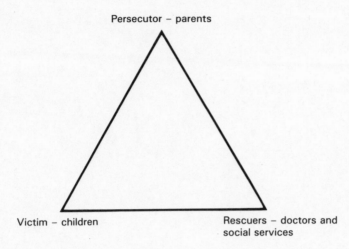

Persecutor – parents

Victim – children

Rescuers – doctors and social services

Figure 10.2

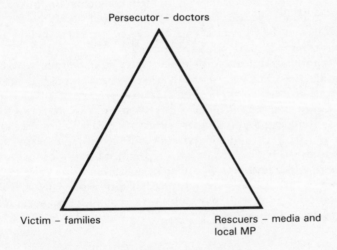

Persecutor – doctors

Victim – families

Rescuers – media and local MP

whole. In this respect Butler-Sloss and her team did a remarkably effective report, avoiding being drawn into the triangle with the hasty throwing of blame and instead bringing good supervisory understanding of the whole situation, in which there are not 'goodies and baddies', but in which there are well-intentioned people on all sides who have made mistakes or been misguided.

One of the key pieces of learning that we would like to see come out of the very painful and costly Cleveland situation is that all staff, even if they are senior paediatricians or social service directors need some form of regular

Figure 10.3

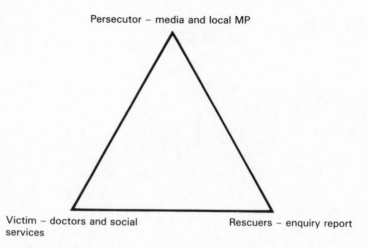

Persecutor – media and local MP

Victim – doctors and social
services

Rescuers – enquiry report

supervision which helps them question their own work in a supportive way, so that they do not retreat into omnipotent conviction on the one hand, or turning a blind eye on the other. Let it not be forgotten that the professionals in the Cleveland case discovered incidents of child abuse that other professionals may well have ignored.

The report rightly called for much better co-operation between all the helping agencies, but what has not been thought through is the need for senior staff in social work, hospitals, general practice, the police force, etc. to be trained not only in good supervision practice, but also in how to supervise complex interdisciplinary situations. We have argued elsewhere in this book that all first-line supervisors should receive training in supervision (see Chapter 7), but we would also recommend that those who supervise from more senior positions within an organization should also be given the opportunity to go on an advanced supervision-skills training that particularly focuses on working with complex organizational and interprofessional situations.

11 Towards a learning culture

In this chapter we will illustrate different types of cultures that are prevalent in helping organizations and how these affect supervision. In the following chapter we will explore how to bring about change in organizations to produce a culture that is more conducive to staff learning and supervision.

In many organizations and professions there is a demand from the front-line workers for better supervision to help them deal with the increasing pressures and complexities that they face daily.

Often the response of the senior managers is to deal with this demand as another problem to be managed in isolation. Responses may include the following:

- sending first-line managers on a short supervision-skills course;
- asking the training department to come up with the answer;
- issuing directives that all staff must have regular supervision.

Let us illustrate what happens to these piecemeal attempts to increase the quality and quantity of supervision. In one social-services department we were called in to run a five-and-a-half-day course for senior staff in residential and day-care establishments. Most of the staff enjoyed the course and personally learnt a lot from it, but their constant complaint was that they were being asked to do better supervision when they either didn't receive any supervision themselves or the supervision they did have was sporadic and poor in quality. Not only did this mean that they had poor role models, but also it inevitably led to a resentment that they were providing for others what they wanted and were not getting for themselves. There would be statements like 'I wish I could get my manager to come on this course,' and 'I have had more supervision on this course than the whole time I have worked for this authority'.

We partly tried to address this problem by teaching the course members how to be pro-active in achieving the supervision they wanted and how to educate their managers (see Chapters 3 and 5). This was partially successful;

in some organizations it has led to more senior managers asking for supervision training themselves. But this is an uphill process, for change in organizations, like water, more easily flows from the top downwards.

Elsewhere we have been brought in to teach supervision in organizations where there is temendous confusion hiding behind the mouthing of statements by senior managers which emphasize how important they think supervision is. In such organizations staff have not known who should be receiving supervision from whom, how often it should happen, or what priority it can be given. Sometimes they would receive double messages – management expecting them to do supervision, but then demanding that they carry an equal case-load to staff who had no supervision responsibilities.

All organizations need a clear statement of policy on supervision. Such a statement needs to state clearly:

Why supervision is important.
Who should receive supervision from *whom*.
When and with what frequency supervision should happen.
How supervision should be carried out – what sort of style and approach.
What supervision should focus on.
What priority supervision should be given in relation to other tasks.

In other organizations we have been brought in, not to deal with the symptoms of poor supervision, but to work with the whole organization in diagnosing the underlying culture that produces these symptoms and devising a strategic organizational change, development and training plan. Only when we have worked in this way has there been a lasting impact on the supervision within an organization, rather than change that is dependent on a few individuals who might up and leave.

Good supervision starts from the top
Supervision needs to be built into the very fabric of an organization

In order to explore how you bring about a much more fundamental change in the culture of an organization, let us pause and ask what is organizational culture?

What is culture?

McLean and Marshall in their workbook, *Working with Cultures: A Workbook for People in Local Government* (1988), quote various writers who have studied organizational cultures:

culture is:

... how things are done around here.

(Ouchi and Johnson 1978)

... values and expectations which organization members come to share.

(Van Maanen and Schein 1979)

... the social glue that holds the organization together.

(Baker 1980)

... the way of thinking, speaking and (inter)acting that characterize a certain group.

(Braten 1983)

... the taken for granted and shared meanings that people assign to their social surroundings.

(Wilkens 1983)

... the collection of traditions, values, policies, beliefs and attitudes that constitute a pervasive context for everything we do and think in an organization.

(McLean and Marshall 1983)

McLean and Marshall (1988) go on to explore how culture is carried not only in the high-profile symbols of an organization such as logos, prestige events and training programmes, but also in the low-profile symbols.

Essentially everything in an organization is symbolic; patterns of meaning in the culture mirrored in multiple forms of expression – in language, relationships, paperwork (or its lack), physical settings ... how meetings are called and conducted, who sits next to whom, who interrupts, what time different topics are given, what lines of reasoning prevail and so on.

Thus the organization's culture of supervision can be seen in the high-profile symbol of its policy about supervision, but can be more accurately seen in its low-profile symbols: where supervision takes place, who supervises, how regular the sessions are, what importance is given to them and what priority they have when time pressures necessitate something's being cancelled.

There can be a split between the high and low cultures which is similar to the distinction that Argyris and Schön (1978) make concerning 'espoused theory' and 'theory in action'. Some social-services departments have a policy with grand phrases about the key importance of supervision and on-going development and support of staff; yet supervision is the first thing to be cancelled when there are staff shortages.

Other writers have referred to the organizational culture as representing the unconscious of the organization, as it is embedded in the ways of experiencing what happens; thus they see culture as less to do with what is done and more to do with how it is viewed, heard and experienced.

Organizational cultures in the helping professions

In working as organizational consultants to a number of health services, social-work departments, probation teams and voluntary organizations, we have come to recognize certain distinct and typical cultures that exist in the helping professions.

We have called these cultures:

A The personal pathology culture
B The bureaucratic culture
C Watch-your-back culture
D Reactive/crisis-driven culture
E The learning/developmental culture

Each of these cultures produces a different attitude and approach to supervision.

A The personal pathology culture   This culture is based on seeing all problems as located in the personal pathology of individuals. It is highly influenced by psychodynamic casework theories, but with little understanding of either group dynamics or how systems function.

If there is a problem in one department's not functioning, the first thing that managers with this cultural set do is to look for the problem person. This is often the head of the department. The belief is that, if we can cure the sick individual, the department will be healthy. If the sick individual does not seem to respond to treatment, then you look for a way of removing him or her.

This approach, that degenerates very quickly into scapegoating, can happen at all levels of the organization. The residential home for children will report that all their troubles would be solved if only they could find a way of moving young Tommy somewhere else. However, when and if they do move Tommy to another home, then Sally becomes the problem child, and so on.

We have also worked with teams where the team has located all its problems in one member. 'If only Jack would take early retirement,' they all sigh. This attitude ensures that they are impotent in addressing the collective team problems as you cannot solve a problem that you do not first own, as in part, yours.

In one large voluntary organization individual homes were elected one at a time to be 'the problem child' of the organization. The unspoken belief was that, if this home could be sorted out, then the whole organization would be problem free!

In this culture supervision can become problem centred and aimed at treating pathology. This can create a subtle form of paranoia in the supervisees who fear that, if they do not keep the focus on the pathology of their clients, they themselves may become 'a suitable case for treatment'. On one of our five-and-a-half-day supervision-skills courses, one head of an old people's home went back to his home to introduce supervision as his mid-course project. He announced in the staff meeting that he was going to introduce supervision and that he was going to start with James. James immediately exclaimed: 'Why pick on me – what have I done wrong?'

In this culture we also find that staff will sometimes say: 'I do not need supervision this week as I do not have any problems.' Team leaders will tell us that they give supervision on an *ad hoc* basis 'when problems arise'. This culture creates the belief that, if you go for supervision, you must have a problem or, more perniciously, there must be something wrong with you.

This attitude is intensified by the policy of giving students the most regular supervision, the new staff the next largest amount, and senior staff no supervision at all. The message in this low-profile symbol is very clear – if you want to get on in this culture, demonstrate that you do not need supervision. Supervision is only for the untrained, inexperienced or needy.

B The bureaucratic culture This form of organization has been extensively written about by Isobel Menzies (1970) in her classic paper on nursing cultures in hospitals entitled *The Functioning of Social Systems as a Defence against Anxiety*. This form of organization is high on task orientation and low on personal relatedness. There are policies and memos to cover all eventualities and all meetings have tight agendas.

In this culture supervision is mostly concerned with checking up that all the tasks have been done correctly. We have worked with team leaders who have arrived at supervision with their staff with an agenda which is like a mechanic's check list. When they have ticked off all the items, the supervision is finished. They may say as they walk out of the door: 'Oh by the way, how are you?' but possibly they will not stay to hear the answer.

For the supervisee the supervision is one of reporting back what they have and have not achieved. Again the culture is problem centred but this time the ethos is that of mechanics rather than sickness and treatment. There is little space for understanding in the rush for tidy answers.

C Watch-your-back-culture This form of organizational culture becomes prevalent where there is either a very politicalized climate or a highly competitive one. Some departments are riven with internal power battles between sub-groups. Sometimes this has been on political or racial grounds, but sometimes it is more to do with cliques and who is on whose side. In this atmosphere much energy goes in ensuring that the other sides do not have all the information for fear of the possibility that they will use what they know against you. Meanwhile you make sure that you use everything you can to expose the other group.

Charles Handy (1976) in his book *Understanding Organizations* points out:

> In all organizations there are individuals and groups competing for
> influence or resources, there are differences of opinion and of values,
> conflicts of priorities and of goals. There are pressure groups and

lobbies, cliques and cabals, rivalries and contests, clashes of personality and bonds of alliance.

Often in the helping professions power and rivalry are denied and then become even more powerful as shadow forces that are not recognized (see Chapter 2).

This form of culture can also develop in a very hierarchical organization where the climate is set that those who 'keep their noses clean' will get promotion. This leads staff to ensure that they cover up any difficulties, inadequacies or problems they are having, as it would be detrimental to share these.

> I have regular meetings with my supervisor, but always steer clear of my problems in coping with my report work. Can I trust her? I need her backing for my career progress, but will she use this sort of thing as evidence against me? There are some painful areas that are never discussed but *need* discussing so much. It is an awful dilemma for me.
>
> (Fineman 1985: 52)

What happens to supervision in this culture depends on who your supervisor is. If you are supervised by one of your own power sub-group, it becomes conspiratorial and falls into discussing how awful the other sides are. If it is with someone who is 'one of them' or a manager you do not trust, then it is centred on covering up, putting a good gloss on the work you have done and making sure you are seen in a good light.

D Reactive/crisis culture   In one of our courses, where we were teaching the archetypal roles of helping (see Chapter 4), one of the course members suggested Superman as an archetypal role that some supervisors play. We were doubtful about this until, on our very next course, there was a very quiet head of a children's home who sat taking notes in the corner. He was dressed more traditionally than the other course members, with a tie and jacket. Added to this, his glasses and studiousness made him seem more like a librarian than a social worker. In the middle of the second day a message arrived for him to say that there was a problem at his home. He jumped up in the middle of the session and seemed to grow before our very eyes. 'I must GO – there is a crisis in my home,' he exclaimed loudly as he swept out of the room. It was clear that this head of home became much more alive when there was a good crisis for him to handle and we are sure that his clients duly obliged by producing regular crises for him to respond to.

We have visited other homes and departments where the staff never have uninterrupted time to meet, as one of them is always responding to the latest crisis. In this type of organization there is never time to reflect properly on the work or the plan ahead, the focus is always on the intensity of the moment. As in the story above, clients pick up this culture and realize that, if you want to get attention around here, produce a crisis.

When we first worked in a half-way house for the adult mentally ill, cutting one's wrists seemed to be contagious. Even those who had no previous record of wrist-cutting seemed to be starting. The staff were always rushing to the local casualty department, holding hastily bandaged arms. Eventually we managed to stem the flood of crises long enough to hold a staff meeting to reflect on this. We realized that those who cut their wrists were getting far more attention than the other residents. We, as a staff group, were perpetuating this particular crisis culture. The staff made it clear to the community that in future the staff would not visit clients in the hospital who had overdosed or cut their wrists and would instead give more attention to the clients who avoided such behaviour. Immediately the number of crises dropped dramatically.

In other organizations staff have told us that the only way to get time with the director is to have a crisis in your section, then the director who is always too busy to see you sends out an urgent summons for you to see him. In another voluntary organization the assistant director would fly in by helicopter and give supervision in the nearest café, pub or in the car, before flying back to 'base'.

In this culture supervision is rarely a high priority and will get cancelled regularly, always for very important reasons. When it does happen, it often creates the atmosphere of being in a tremendous rush and having to solve problems in a hurry before the next wave or onslaught bears down upon us.

E *The learning/developmental culture* This is clearly the culture in which supervision most flourishes. It is built on a belief system that a great deal of social work and indeed counselling and therapy is about creating the environment and relationships in which clients learn about themselves and their environment, in a way that leaves them with more options than they arrived with. Further it believes that social workers, counsellors and therapists, etc., are best able to facilitate others to learn if they are supported in constantly learning and developing themselves. An organization that is learning and developing right from the top of the organization to the bottom is far more likely to be meeting the needs of the clients, because it is also meeting the needs of staff. One of the authors has written extensively about the learning culture elsewhere (Hawkins 1979, 1980, 1986) but we will summarize the key attributes of such a culture and how they affect supervision.

- Learning and development are seen as continuous life-long processes. Thus in such a culture the most experienced and the most senior staff ensure that they have on-going supervision or consultancy and do not see supervision as just for the untrained and inexperienced. The actions of the senior managers speak louder than their policy statements and it is important that they conspicuously exemplify the learning culture by, among other things, having supervision themselves.
- A learning culture emphasizes the potential that all the different work situations have for learning, both individually and collectively.

- Problems and crises are seen as important opportunities for learning and development, both individually and organizationally. Major crises are seen as growth points and the culture is one where it is safe to take risks, for failures are seen as events to be learnt from, not as evidence for the prosecution of individuals.
- Good practice emerges neither from an action culture that is always dealing with the latest problems and crises, nor from a theorizing culture that is withdrawing from the real issues to draw up theoretical policy papers. Good practice comes from staff, teams and departments that are well balanced in all parts of the learning cycle, that goes from *action*, to *reflection*, to *new thinking*, to *planning* and then back to *action* (see Kolb, Rubin and McIntyre 1971 and Juch 1983).
- This means that supervision needs to avoid rushing for quick solutions, but also to avoid getting lost in abstract theorizing. Rather it must start with reflecting on the concrete experience and try to make sense of this in a way that allows the experience to challenge one's own way of seeing and thinking about the world. But supervision must not stay at the point of new insight, but rather use this new insight to generate new options, evaluate these options and choose what new strategy to put into operation. This new action then needs to be reviewed in the following supervision so that the learning cycle does not become a one circuit process.
- Learning becomes an important value in its own right. Supervisors carry the attitude 'How can I help these supervisees to maximize their learning in this situation so that they can help the client learn too?'; rather than the attitude 'How can I ensure that the supervisees make no mistakes and do it the way I think is right?'
- Individuals and teams take time out to reflect on their effectiveness, learning and development. In a learning culture there are team-development sessions or 'away-days' (see Brown 1984). There are also staff appraisals that are not based on the senior's grading the staff member on performance, but involve a co-operative process of the staff members' appraising their own development, their own strengths and weaknesses and then receiving feedback on and refinement of their own appraisal from both their peers and their senior.

  A good appraisal system will focus, not just on performance, but also what the staff member has learnt, how they have developed and how their learning and development can best proceed and be nurtured in the forthcoming period.
- There would be a high level of on-going feedback, both from peers and between levels within the organization. Also feedback would be encouraged from those with whom the work team or organization relate: customers, other helping organizations, professional networks, politicians, etc.
- Time and attention will be given to the transition of individuals: how new staff are welcomed and inducted into the team and organization: how they

are helped to go through leaving and changes in status within the organization. Time would be given to this in both team and individual supervision.

- Roles will be regularly reviewed and negotiated. They will be allocated not just on the basis of efficiency, but also on the potential that each role provides as a learning opportunity for its incumbent. This would include the role of supervisor which would not just be allocated to the automatic person in the hierarchy.
- In such a culture the learning does not reside just in individuals, who may up and leave, but it is ensured that the learning happens at the team and organizational levels and is both recorded and lived in the developing culture.

(For further information on the learning culture and the research on which it is based see Hawkins 1986.)

Conclusion

In this chapter we have tried to show how supervision is not just an event, but an on-going process which should permeate the culture of any effective helping organization. Nearly all organizational cultures are a mix of several of the organizational types that we have illustrated and caricatured. We have yet to meet an organization that fully lives up to the ideals of the learning culture. Some organizations do go a long way along the road of creating such an environment. One example, which alas no longer functions in the same way, is Dingleton Hospital in Scotland. How it functioned and gradually became more of a learning culture can be read in Jones (1982).

In the next chapter we will explore how you can go about changing the culture and structure of your own team and organization, so that you will have the tools to create more of a learning culture in your own workplace.

12 Bringing about change in teams and organizations

Although this is not a book on organizational change and development, we would like to look at some basic principle in bringing about change in whole organizations, for three reasons:

- We do not want to limit the concept of supervision just to students and junior staff, but see it as an important element of the work of staff at all levels, right up to chief executives. One of the key tasks of senior staff in supervising organizations is to manage organizational change in both a smooth and creative way.
- Supervision must also not be limited to helping an individual monitor and learn from their own work. Teams, departments and whole organizations need to be supervised in order to learn and develop from their experience.
- Those staff who have taken on the task of introducing supervision into an organization, or part of an organization, where it previously has not existed, need some basic skills in organizational change in order to carry out this task.

Types of change

Not all types of change are of the same level. Golembiewski (1976) has provided us with a simple model of distinguishing between different levels of change.

Alpha change – first-order change   These are simple, routine and minor changes. In one's home life, examples of this would be decorating a room, replanting the garden, etc. At work it might involve getting a new colleague, starting a new group or a change in supervisor.

Beta change – second-order change These have more general implications and involve a shift in the framework within which alpha change happens. This might be a change in one's job or house. At work it might involve a change in working practices, the introduction of supervision, or a change in how supervision happens.

Gamma change – third-order change This is a radical change involving a fundamental shift of assumptions and values and hence a change in the framework from which choices of beta and alpha changes are made. In non-work life this might be having children, change in marital status, religious conversion or a serious illness. At work it might involve a major shift in the overall task of the organization, or a change in the organizational culture.

When is organizational gamma change necessary?

Those involved in organizational change need to be clear about the level of change they are embarking on. Health departments and local authorities regularly go through structural re-organizations, in fact, one social-services director told us that, among his peers, it was considered that you had not really come of age as a director until you had handled your first major departmental re-organization! In most departments much more energy is given to re-organizing the structure of the department than to looking at the culture of the department and the separate sub-cultures within it. Yet a new structure will not root and flourish if it does not fit with the culture in which it is planted. So many re-organizations try and seed new plants without preparing the soil and ensuring that it is suitable for the intended growth. Another analogy is that it is like trying to change people's behaviour and mode of operating without looking at the reasons they operate the way they do in the first place.

Yet it is also important not to engage on the more stressful level of gamma change when the needs of the organization, department or team are only for beta or alpha change.

Gamma change is necessary when an organization is going through a major developmental transition. A number of large voluntary helping organizations have had major problems in working through a growth transition. They had mostly started as charismatically founded radical organizations for providing a new form of care for a particular client group, where the staff functioned as a very committed family. Everyone not only knew everyone else, but they were all involved in each other's work. With the success of such an organization comes a very rapid growth in size. Suddenly the family atmosphere begins to go. There is a need to have more formal meeting structures, communication channels and procedures. Splits develop between the 'founders' and the 'newcomers'. The newcomers often want the organization to become more professional, whilst the founders resent the loss of 'missionary zeal' and feel the newcomers are trying to take over their 'baby'.

Gamma change is also necessary when the environment in which the work happens changes very rapidly. Sudden changes in funding policy from central or local government can necessitate the need for helping an organization to undertake major change. Changes in ways of thinking about care can also create the need for a major rethink. In Britain there are a number of child-care agencies which were built up in the days of large children's homes, with Victorian ethics and Christian values. In the last twenty years there has been a major move away from seeing this as a suitable approach for dealing with children in care. With the rapid growth of adoption and fostering, alongside the rapid increase in the cost of labour and of running large properties, the bottom has fallen out of the residential-children's-home market. These large charities as well as residential departments within social services, have had to go through a process of gamma change.

The enormous upsurge in the awareness of sexual abuse is necessitating gamma change for social services and organizations like the National Society for the Prevention of Cruelty to Children. The enormous upsurge in prison referrals is necessitating gamma change in the prison service. New diseases like AIDS call for major change in a wide variety of helping organizations; in the health service, in organizations that work with drug addicts, in counselling organizations and in the hospice movement.

Political change puts the future of local government, as it presently exists, in the balance. The growth of private medicine is beginning radically to affect the health services. No longer can staff work in the helping professions and ignore the outside world. Change is the only thing that will remain constant in the period of development and Plant (1987) repeats the warning previously made by Reg Revans (1982). 'Organizations that do not learn at a faster rate than their environment changes will eventually die.' Or as Revans expressed it in a formula:

$$L \cong C$$

Learning must equal or be greater than the amount of environmental change.

Factors influencing change

Clearly the success of helping organizations is increasingly influenced by their ability to manage and cope with change. There are certain factors which make an organization more ready to cope successfully with change. These are:

- clear organizational vision and overall task;
- a strong set of organizational values;

- organizational goals that are clearly stated;
- good and reliable levels of consultation;
- communication throughout the organization that is quick and clear;
- decisions that are made, as far as possible, by those who have first-hand knowledge and are closest to the problem;
- the organizational procedures are largely determined by the task;
- personal and ideological differences are tackled openly;
- people are rewarded for developing subordinates and building work teams, and not just for immediate output;
- individuality is respected and maintained;
- minorities are respected and listened to;
- there is a continual conscious attempt by everyone to learn from experience.

Resistances to change

However, even in an organization that achieved a large amount of the above pre-conditions, change would still create resistance. The difference is that in such an organization the resistance to the change would have a much better chance of being successfully worked through.

Resistance to change and unwillingness to engage in new behaviour are fuelled by a number of factors:

Fear of the unknown
Lack of information
Misinformation
Historical factors
Threat to core skills and competence
Threat to status
Threat to power base
No perceived benefits
Low trust in the organization
Poor relationships
Fear of failure
Fear of looking stupid
Reluctance to experiment
Custom bound
Reluctance to let go
Strong peer group norms.

(Plant 1987)

Kurt Lewin (1952) adapted from physics into the field of human relations the law that says: '*Every force creates its equal and opposite force.*' He developed the concept of force-field analysis, that the more you push for change the more resistance you create. This is clearly seen in the following example taken from an intergroup negotiation:

Group A bring three arguments to support their case. Group B bring three arguments to support theirs. Group A, instead of looking for common ground, make the mistake of adding three more reasons why they are right. Group B immediately double the number of reasons for their viewpoint and at the same time raise their voices. Group A raise their decibel level by almost the same amount and start ridiculing the case of group B who, surprise, surprise, reply in kind.

When you try to create any form of change, be it in an individual worker or a whole organization and you meet resistance, pushing harder for the change just creates more resistance. Lewin suggests that, instead, you stop and attend to what is creating the impasse. You draw a line down the page and on one side you put all the forces that are supporting the change. On the other side you show all the forces that are resisting the change. Then in order to shift the status quo, you find ways of attending to the resistances in a way that would meet the underlying needs that are fuelling them. If you can honour and redirect the resistance, the change will happen without having to use greater effort.

Here is an example of a force-field analysis of a situation in which a new team leader is trying to introduce supervision into a team where it has previously not existed.

Table 12.1   Introducing individual supervision for the first time into a team

Driving forces	Restraining forces
Staff want more support	Fear of being assessed
Enthusiasm of team leader	Paranoia about what the team leader's motives are
Team Leader is clear about his goals	Previous bad experience of supervision by some team members
'Time for me'	Thinking that supervision is to do with failure
Staff feel supervision may help Team Leader understand their problems better	Very time consuming

In this situation an increase in the enthusiasm of the team leader about supervision or even his trying to convince team members about how good it would be for them would tend only to increase their paranoia about what he was trying to get them to do. Alternatively it might give them the sense that they really must be in a bad way for him to be so insistent that they need supervision. The wise team leader would instead look at ways of honouring and redirecting their resistances. Perhaps he would give them time to talk about their previous bad experiences of supervision or would engage them in planning the best and most time-efficient supervision system for this particular team.

In dealing with resistance it is also useful to realize that resistance often changes over time and can go through various stages. Fink, Beak and Taddeo (1971) postulate four phases through which groups or organizations will pass in response to change: shock; defensive retreat; acknowledgement; adaption and change.

In *shock*, interpersonal relations become fragmented, decision making becomes paralysed and communication confused. This leads to *defensive retreat*: individuals become self-protective, teams retreat into their own enclaves and become inward looking, decision making becomes more autocratic and communication more ritualized. In the *acknowledgement* phase individuals and teams begin to own that there are things that need changing and more support and confrontation are present. When the fourth stage of *adaption and change* is reached, relations become more interdependent, there is more communication between individuals and across team boundaries, there is more willingness to explore and experiment with other ways of operating, and communication becomes more direct and open.

Thus it can be counter-productive to give people your marvellous scenarios for their future. They need to be involved in the thinking through and planning of the changes so that they have the opportunity to react, then understand the need for change and then adapt to the future necessities. It is very easy to think that because you have worked through the issues and come up with a good solution, other people need only to accept the rightness of the solution and do not need to go through the thinking process.

Phases in bringing about organizational change

The first step to changing a culture is to become clearer about what the culture is. Often organizational chiefs are so anxious to rush into what the culture 'ought to be' that they do not stay long enough finding out what it is. The most useful rule in any change is: '*Start from where you are.*'

There is a basic order of phases that the change process needs to go through if the change is going to be effective. However they should not be considered as a linear ladder of success, but rather as a circular process, with a constant need to return again to the beginning stage in the next cycle of development. These phases are:

1 Recognizing the need and mobilizing the commitment to change.
2 Exploring the present state of the organization and its culture.
3 Building a vision for change.
4 Seeding the new vision.
5 Developing an organizational strategy that will take the organization forward in a way that is congruent both with its vision and the changing external realities.

6 Realigning the organizational structure, methods and roles in the best way to carry out the new strategy.
7 Reviewing what has been created and re-entering the next cycle of change and development.

We will now look in more detail at each of these stages.

1 Recognizing the need and mobilizing the commitment to change

We mentioned earlier in the book the maxim that you cannot solve a problem that you do not own, and in organizational change it is no good trying to change an organization, department or team that does not recognize it needs to change. The impetus for change must come from within. External agents, be they more senior managers, supervisors or external consultants, can help the organization or department to bring to the surface its own perceived strengths and problems; its unutilized capacities and resources; the environmental changes that are acting upon it and its dissatisfaction with the status quo. What they cannot do is create the commitment to change that must come from within.

It is also necessary to get commitment to the change process from those who have power or authority in relation to the department or organization which wants to change. Change in one part of an organization has an effect on the other parts of an organization and can create in those above or to the side resistance which may lead to the change effort being sabotaged. It is important before embarking on any change programme to map out all the interested parties (those who will be affected by the change process) and consider how they can be brought on board.

Bob Garratt, who works with change in international commercial organizations, suggests (1987) asking three questions to ensure that you maximize the political support for your change effort from the wider network:

> Who knows? – who has the information about the problem? Not opinions, views, half-truths, official policies, but hard facts which will determine the dimensions of the problem.
> Who cares? – who has the emotional investment in getting change made? Again, this is not who talks about the problem but who is involved in and committed to the outcome. These are often the people directly involved in and committed to the outcome ...
> Who can? – who has the power to reorder resources so that changes occur? ... who, when faced with facts, commitment and energy, has the power to say 'Yes'.

External consultants can also help organizations in this first process to unfreeze the closed systems, the tightly held assumptions and the unwritten rules, and to create a window of opportunity through heightened awareness and through expanding the realm of possibilities. By being an outsider the consultant can avoid being trapped in the limiting assumptions that constrain the horizons of possibility within an organization.

2 Exploring the present state of the organization and its culture

In exploring the present state of the organization it is important to place organizations in their historical and environmental setting. Several key writers have written about the typical organizational developmental stages and how the key periods of change are when an organization is in transition from one developmental stage to another. (Lievegoed 1973; Blake, Avis and Mouton 1966; Plant 1987). In working with an organizational transition it is important to honour the previous culture, strategy and structure as being right for the previous stage of development, while recognizing that the environment and the times have changed, and the organization must change as well.

Having explored the present state of some organizations, through an organizational workshop, away-day, organizational audit or other means, the organization may conclude that the necessary changes are only at an alpha or beta level. That they are not at a time of organizational transition, but just need to improve their functioning within their present organizational framework.

However, for some organizations it will become clear that a gamma change is necessary. For such a change to be successfully carried out, the present organizational culture needs to be carefully examined.

In the previous chapter we explained how the organizational culture is unconscious; this means that we are faced with the difficulty of how do we become conscious of our unconscious and how do we see our own way of looking? The discipline that has taught us the most about accessing the unconscious is psychotherapy and many of the discoveries in the field of individual therapy can be applied to uncovering the unconscious layers of an organization.

McLean (1986) talks about three ways to access an organisation's culture: *enactment, estrangement, exemplification.*

In the chapter on groupwork we showed how group sculpting can be used to explore the dynamics of a group or team. This is an *enactment* technique and can also be used to explore the dynamics of an organization.

We also gave an example of using *estrangement*, through a fantasy of becoming someone foreign to your group or organization and recording the things you notice which you normally take for granted. Often newcomers to an organization can see the culture more easily than those who are 'encultured' within it. As the Chinese proverb says: 'The last to know about the sea is a fish.'

Another way to carry out estrangement is to think back to when you first joined the organization – what struck you as strange or unusual? – what impressed you? – how did you learn how to behave in order to belong in this new society?

We also become more aware of our national culture after we have been abroad and partaking in a very different culture, so one way to get insight into your own work culture is to visit one or more parallel organizations and see how they are similar to and different from your own.

Accessing the culture of a organization through the approach of *exemplification* can be done by looking at what people, events, rituals, phrases, words etc., exemplify the organization. McLean and Marshall (1988) ask who are the heroes/heroines, villains and fools in the stories that are told within the organization. Most organizations develop their own folklore – stories that are repeatedly told to newcomers about past events; jokes that often recur.

When working as consultant to the Simon Community, which is a large charity working with the down and outs of London, one of us paid particular attention to the rituals which were such a central part of the community's way of life. However, the rituals that had been developed by the charismatic founder Anton Wallich-Clifford, no longer exemplified the living culture. The rituals survived as the community could not free itself from the ghost of their founder. There were two cultures, the one that was kept going in memory of 'how it used to be' which was exemplified in the formal rituals, and a sub-culture of how the members of the community now operated which was exemplified in the informal ways of operating within the community.

Just surfacing the culture can lead to some degree of change. Individuals and organizations may suddenly realize that they do not have to carry on with the same beliefs and ways of working that have become institutionalized. Their new awareness leads to greater choice.

Having surfaced an awareness of their culture, an organization can move on to exploring how they wish this culture to shift. One way of starting this process is known as 'three-way sorting' (George, Hawkins and McLean 1988). The team or organization may have generated a great amount of data about their culture from carrying out the above exercises; they are then asked to create three new lists.

- What lies at the heart; the core values; the root metaphor etc? What needs to be safeguarded and nurtured as the organization moves on?
- What can be discarded, is no longer appropriate and has outlived its usefulness? What is the excess baggage that is slowing down change?
- What needs to be incorporated; acquired; done differently – how does the change represent a time of possibility and opportunity?

This exercise represents the first step in moving into creating a cultural shift and building a new vision which is the next process.

3 Building a vision for the future

Many organizational consultants used to believe that the fundamental step in working with an organization was to get its 'primary task' and its overall objectives clear. However, more recent writings and research on managers and organizations have shown that clarity of purpose is not enough and that objectives need to be linked to underlying values and purpose, if the new objectives are to take root and fundamental attitudes change. Another way of saying this is that it is no good changing objectives unless you shift the culture of the organization as well.

Vision is a sense of how small, daily events link to larger values. Managers who communicate vision are able to say why the work of the agency or team is important in the larger scheme of things. They comfortably link small mundane jobs and problems to the wider issues of the organization and its overall direction. They are able to use the helicopter skills to see a problem in its context and their sense of wider purpose will tend to inspire those around them. Here is an example:

> In recent work with a county-council social-work department, the senior management team were helped to reconnect with their fundamental values by being asked to remember back to when they were first in the helping professions and to discover the values that meant most to them, the people whose work inspired them, and what most motivated them in their work. Having recorded some of these early values they were then asked to look to their present work and answer the same three questions. Finally they were asked to look to the future and consider what kind of department and values would they want to pass on to the director and assistant directors who came after them (they were all, but one, within five years of retiring).
>
> From their three lists they were asked to choose two or three key values they would like to see incorporated in the core values of the department. These were listed on large sheets of paper. At this stage it is important to find which of these values has the most commitment to it from the whole team. To do this we use the Rozel technique (George, Hawkins and McLean 1988). Each of the core-value statements is voted on by the group. There are four possible ways of voting:
>
> - a hand on your heart means 'I not only agree with that but it has my passionate commitment';
> - 'both hands on your lap means 'I can live with that';
> - both hands on your head means 'I either do not understand that or I disagree';
> - one hand raised in the air means 'over my dead body' and one person voting this way acts as a veto on the suggestion.
>
> Any statement that gets a complete heart vote is clearly a core value that has maximum commitment and should appear high up in any draft vision statement. Any statement that either has more laps than hearts or any head votes needs to be further discussed and either omitted or amended. (Several senior management teams have amended this voting system for their ordinary meetings.)

In the further development of such a vision statement, a team or organization should not aim for constraining 'commandments set in stone', but rather guiding principles that give clear purpose and direction. One senior management team had them written in felt-tip pen on a large sheet of paper on the director's wall. It was clear from both the heading and the way they were written that they were a working vision that could both be developed and also be added to by others.

4 Seeding the new vision

If one part of an organization develops a new vision, it is important that they do not go straight out and try and evangelize their vision to the rest of the organization. A vision of a new culture cannot be conveyed by written directives, but is carried through the actions of those who hold it. The team needs to answer the question: 'What actions or new behaviour would conspicuously exemplify the new culture we wish to create?'

In the last chapter we described the high-profile and low-profile symbols which carry the nature of the culture; it is essential that the new vision is exemplified in both types of symbols. Some helping organizations have concentrated on changing their name, their logo or have had the director make troop-rallying speeches to all the staff, but there has been no accompanying change in how the director is seen to act in his daily work, or in what behaviour is rewarded.

You can also look at what intermediate structures would act as carriers of the new culture. Rather than invent a new permanent structure for the whole organization, it is better to set up time-limited task or project groups that will not only work on producing new ways of operating, but also endeavour to act in tune with the new hoped-for culture. For example, if two of the key values of the vision were to have more participation in decision making and to have a better gender balance in the organization's management structure, it would be important that the task groups were selected conspicuously to exemplify these values.

It is also essential that, if a senior management team develops their vision of the organization, they then open up the space for other parts of the organization to create their own vision, both for their own section and for what their section would like to see reflected in the overall vision. Only then is it possible to produce a vision that is grounded in the whole organization and provides a meta-vision that links the organization's various sub-cultures.

5 Developing an organizational strategy that will take the organization forward in a way that is congruent both with its vision and the changing external realities

The next stage is to turn the vision into a strategy that gives more detailed direction to the next period of development. This should link back to the values and vision that have been agreed upon, but also give clear statements about action that will be taken, by whom and in what time sequence.

To help organizations do this, it is possible to ask staff to carry out a guided fantasy in which they travel forward in time, one, two, or even five years. In this fantasy they can look at what is then happening both within the whole organization, their part of it, and also in the wider environment that impinges on them. What will be different? What conditions will they have had to adapt to? Will they still be with the organization, etc? Sometimes groups find it helpful to produce both positive and negative scenarios of their future.

The material that derives from this exercise can then be worked on, with brain-storming and problem-solving techniques creatively to produce an action strategy that is owned by the key staff whose energy and commitment will have to make it happen.

Any strategy that is produced is then related back to the vision and values that have previously been articulated. There are two approaches to producing a critique of the strategy – the Langford model and the Brandenburg Concerto technique (George, Hawkins and McLean 1988).

The Langford model   Each part of the strategy is presented by various members of the team and is then criticized by three devil's advocates. The first looks at how far the process of developing the strategy has been in line with the values and vision that the organization is trying to espouse. The second looks at the content and how far the strategy is taking the organization towards or away from the vision. The third critic is looking at how the strategy is going to be implemented. Is there a congruence between what is being said and how it is being said? Is the medium carrying the message?

The Brandenburg Concerto   In this approach the strategy is criticized by three or more team members who have adopted roles from which to listen and respond to the strategy. For example, when a local authority department had produced its draft strategy, one member listened and responded in the role of a service user, another as a basic-grade staff member, a third as a ratepayer and the fourth as a member of the relevant council committee. This immediately made clear some of the areas that had not been considered and some of the conflicts that would lie ahead in taking foward this strategy.

6 Realigning the organizational structure, methods and roles to best carry out the new strategy

It is only when the overall strategy for the next year or more is in place that decisions can be made about how to reorganize the structure of the organization, how roles and job descriptions should be shifted around, how the meeting structure should be changed and how to create better channels of communication.

On each of these issues it is important to check back that the solution is in line with the values, vision and strategy to which the organization is committed. Once again a version of the Langford approach or the Brandenburg Concerto can be used.

7 Reviewing what has been created and re-entering the next cycle of change and development

In order to ensure that the process is not linear or a one-off event, there needs to be a review of the new organizational culture built into the process. In this review the new culture can be accessed in the ways illustrated above and from this further developments can be envisioned and planned.

Change and the learning culture

These methods of helping a centre, team or whole organization look at its culture provide a way of a collective group's learning about itself. A healthy supervision culture cannot be limited to providing opportunities for clients and staff to learn about themselves but must also provide an approach for teams and organizations to learn about themselves collectively. Organizations need to learn as well as individual people.

It is also important that organizations develop a framework that links processes at the micro-level, such as the individual client, or group meeting, or single event, with processes at an organizational level, such as the whole centre, department or organization. In a learning culture all forms of change, whether they be the rehabilitation of one client or the reorganization of a whole department, are looked at from a consistent perspective.

We have mainly described the processes of organizational change on the macro-level of a whole organization, but the same processes apply to trying to change a probation team or a youth club. The processes also apply for anyone who is trying to introduce supervision at any level or within any of the helping professions. For, like any other reorganization, if you try to seed a new plant without first creating and preparing the soil, it will never take root. Good supervision happens where there is a good learning culture. Whether you work in a small unit or as director of a large national helping organization, if you want to introduce or improve supervision in your work-place, then the seven phases of changing the culture should ideally be used.

13 Conclusion: The wounded helper

Until recently there was a GP in Glasgow whose patients would queue up for over three hours to see any other doctor but him. His lack of caring and sensitivity and his boredom with patients he had 'looked after' for years, eventually alienated them. Until, that is, his grandson was found to have leukaemia and slowly, through his own hurt and pain and anger, he was able to touch his patients again. Why is it that often, the very people we expect to understand the anguish of pain, illness and maybe death, often turn their professional, and for that matter human, backs until perhaps such time as they themselves have similar traumas?

(*Guardian* 'Society tomorrow', 1 October 1986)

In many helping professions, from social work to alternative health practitioners, from doctors to teachers, and from nurses to marriage-guidance counsellors, the hardest work, and yet also the simplest, is to meet the clients in their pain. Some professionals, like the doctor mentioned in the *Guardian* quotation above, are in flight from their own pain and therefore have to construct enormous barriers between themselves and the pain of their clients. Other professionals take care of their own distress through projecting it into their clients and needing to make their clients better. When the client gets too close, the doctor may reach for his prescription pad, the social worker may give advice, the probation officer plan a contract, and each in his or her own way is trying to take the pain away. Sometimes this is necessary as the pain and hurt in the client have become unmanageable for them and they need temporary relief before returning to face that wound within themselves. However, professionals can reach too quickly for ways of making it better, for their own needs, for it is they rather than the clients who cannot bear to sit with the pain and distress. We often remind supervisees that their clients have lived with this pain for many, many years and the clients' ability to tolerate the pain is probably much greater than theirs.

There are many therapists who have shown the way to 'stay with' what is happening. Winnicott writes: 'If only we (therapists) can wait (and resist a

personal need to interpret) the patient arrives at understanding creatively.'
(Winnicott 1971).

There is so much pain and hurt in the world that, if we get caught into
believing, we have to make it all better heroically; we are setting ourselves
up to be overwhelmed and to burn out quickly. However, if we react to this
reality with professional defensiveness, we may treat the symptoms, but we
fail to meet and support the human beings who are communicating through
these symptoms. The middle ground entails being on the path of facing our
own shadow, our own fear, hurt and distress, and taking responsibility for
ensuring that we practise what we preach. This means managing our own
support system, finding friends and colleagues who will not just reassure us
but also challenge our defences, and finding a supervisor or supervision
group who will not collude in trying to see who can be most potent with
ways of curing the client but will attend to how we are stuck in relating to
the full truth of those with whom we work.

Often we have had the experience of working in supervision with a
supervisee who is very stuck in knowing what to do next with the client. In the
supervision supervisees may start by looking for better answers and techniques
for managing the client out there, but the real shift comes when they start to
look at their own responses to the client. They might find that they are
frightened of the aspect of themselves that the client represents; that the client
reminds them of someone in their own lives, restimulates a past distress within
them, or produces a strong counter-reaction to their problems.

When this has been explored, supervisees will often report at their next
session, with some surprise, that they did not need to use any of the new
strategies for managing the client, for 'It was as if the client had heard the
supervision and had arrived at the next session much freer.' Some people
may term this 'absent healing', but at a much simpler level we would believe
that the client very quickly responds to an awareness that the helper is now
ready to hear what the client needs to share.

Jampolsky (1979) tells a story where his own readiness through self-
supervision made a direct and immediate impact on a client:

> The episode took place in 1951 at Stanford Lane Hospital, which was
> then located in San Francisco.
>
> The situation was one in which I felt trapped and immobilized by
> fear. I was feeling emotional pain, and thought I was threatened with
> potential physical pain. The past was certainly colouring my
> perception of the present ...
>
> I was called in at 2 a.m. one Sunday morning to see a patient on the
> locked psychiatric ward who had suddenly gone berserk. The patient,
> whom I had not seen before, had been admitted the previous
> afternoon with a diagnosis of acute schizophrenia. About ten minutes
> before I saw him, he had removed the wooden moulding from around
> the door. I looked through the small window in the door, and saw a
> man six feet four inches tall weighing 280 pounds. He was running

around the room nude, carrying this large piece of wood with nails sticking out, and talking gibberish. I really didn't know what to do. There were two male nurses, both of whom seemed scarcely five feet tall, who said, 'We will be right behind you, Doc.' I didn't find that reassuring.

As I continued to look through the window, I began to recognize how scared the patient was, and then it began to trickle into my consciousness how scared I was. All of a sudden it occurred to me that he and I had a common bond that might allow for unity – namely, that we were both scared.

Not knowing what else to do, I yelled through the thick door, 'My name is Dr Jampolsky and I want to come in and help you, but I'm scared. I'm scared that I might get hurt, and I'm scared you might get hurt, and I can't help wondering if you aren't scared too.' With this, he stopped his gibberish, turned around and said, 'You're goddam right I'm scared.'

I continued yelling to him, telling him how scared I was, and he was yelling back how scared he was. In a sense we became therapists to each other. As we talked our fear disappeared and our voices calmed down. He then allowed me to walk in alone, talk with him and give him some oral medication and leave.

In this book we have started with examining motives for wanting to help others. We see this as the beginning of self-supervision, the ability and the desire to question one's practice. We have, in the first instance, concentrated on some of the less straightforward motives – not because we believe that people are fundamentally devious, but because a thorough examination of motives can help us to be more honest with ourselves and therefore our clients.

From this examination of motives and the need for commitment to continual emotional growth we explored, in Chapter 3, ways of taking charge of our own needs for support and supervision. We emphasized that there were skills that could be learnt in being an effective supervisee that formed part of being an effective supervisor.

In the second section of this book (Chapters 4–7) we introduced many of the issues involved in being a supervisor. The maps and models that are available in understanding the process and framework of supervision; the boundaries of the relationship; some of the skills needed for effective supervision and ways of establishing training courses for different types of supervisors. Throughout this exploration we have not confined ourselves to one approach, but rather presented the various choices and issues that each supervisor needs to consider in the process of establishing a personal style of supervising. The style chosen needs to be appropriate to the profession, the organization within which the supervision takes place, the level of development and the needs of the supervisee, and also the personality of the supervisor.

In the third section of the book we explored supervision in groups, peer groups and work teams. We examined the advantages and disadvantages of these forms of supervision and also ways of working with the group dynamics and team development.

However, supervision does not take place in isolation and we devoted the fourth part of the book to looking at the organizational context in which supervision takes place. We outlined ways of looking at the 'culture' of organizations and some of the typical cultures that prevail within helping organizations. We looked at the importance of establishing a learning culture to provide the climate that supports and sustains supervision, not just in formal sessions, but also as an integral part of the working context.

In writing this book we have stressed the need to integrate both the emotional and the rational, the personal and the organizational, and the educative, supportive and managerial aspects of supervision. This integration inevitably provides a creative tension that has to be constantly understood and worked with.

Our ways of working have both followed and developed the process-centred approach to supervision which was first suggested by Ekstein and Wallerstein (1972) in which the emphasis is on the interaction between client, worker and supervisor. In this approach we avoid the polarization of focusing solely on the client or the supervisee; instead we focus on how the relationship between the worker and the client emerges in the supervision session, both in the content brought by the worker and in the process that emerges between worker and supervisor.

Throughout the book we are aware that we have been acting on certain assumptions – namely that supervision is worthwhile. We have occasionally cited evidence that job satisfaction is related to receiving good supervision, quoted cases where shifts have occurred through supervision, and included both theory and personal accounts. But ultimately as Rioch, Coulter and Weinberger (1976) suggest.

> There is no way to escape the fact that in (helping others) we are not really able to count the cost or measure the results ... The truth is that we are performing an act of faith – faith in our clients, and the workers we supervise. It does not really matter that this is occasionally misplaced or that we fail more than once in spite of experience or skill. Like other kinds of faith, this one persists although it is based on things unseen and unheard. Essentially, it is faith in the value of truth, not so much truth with a capital 'T' that would reveal to us the nature of ultimate reality, but truth as the opposite of the small daily self deceptions or the large paranoid delusions that destroy people's respect for themselves and each other.

This commitment to truth, we believe, is more important than all techniques and theoretical approaches. Eventually there come times when we have to act from some deep place within ourselves – perhaps induced by a crisis or a client who tests us out or who is very similar to us. At these times it may be that the right course of action is something which goes against all our previous convictions.

> There were rules in the monastery, but the master always warned against the tyranny of the law. 'Obedience keeps the rules', he would say, 'but Love knows when to break them'.
>
> (De Mello 1985)

Good supervision, like love, we believe, cannot be taught. The understanding, maps and techniques that we provide in this book cannot and, perhaps should not, protect supervisee and supervisor alike from times of self-questioning and doubt. At these times it is the quality of the relationship that has already been established between them that contains the supervisee in times of crisis and doubt. How we personally relate to our supervisors and supervisees is far more important than mere skills, for all techniques need to be embedded in a good relationship. We agree with Hunt (1986) when she says:

> It seems that whatever approach or method is used in the end it is the quality of the relationship between supervisor and supervisee that determines whether supervision is effective or not.
>
> (Hunt 1986)

This relationship provides the container for the helper and forms part of the therapeutic triad we referred to in Chapter 1. It is a relationship that, like any other, will have its difficulties. But without it we believe the work with clients is incomplete.

As Dr Margaret Tonnesmann emphasized in her lecture at the fourth annual conference to commemorate the work of Donald Winnicott:

> The human encounter in the helping profession is inherently stressful. The stress aroused can be accommodated and used for the understanding of our patients and clients. But our emotional responsiveness will wither if the human encounter cannot be contained within the institutions in which we work. Defensive manoeuvres will then become operative and these will prevent healing, even if cure can be maintained by scientific methods, technical skills and organizational competence. By contrast, if we can maintain contact with the emotional reality of our clients and ourselves then the human encounter can facilitate not only a healing experience, but also an enriching experience for them and for us.

A good supervisory relationship is the best way we know to ensure that we stay open to ourselves and our clients.

Bibliography

Albott, W. (1984). 'Supervisory characteristics and other sources of supervision variance', *The Clinical Supervisor*, 2, 27–41.

Aldridge, L. (1982). 'Construction of a Scale for the Rating of Supervisors of Psychology'. Unpublished Masters thesis Auburn University. USA.

Argyris, C. (1982). *Reasoning, Learning and Action*. San Francisco, Josey Bass.

Argyris, C. and Schön, D. (1978), *Organizational Learning*. Reading Mass., Addison-Wesley.

Badaines, J. (1985). 'Supervision: methods and issues', *Self and Society: European Journal of Humanistic Psychology*, XIII (2), 77–81.

Belbin, M. (1981). *Management Teams: Why they Succeed or Fail*. London, Heinemann.

Bennis, W. and Nanus, B. (1985). *Leaders: The Strategies for Taking Charge*. New York, Harper & Row.

Bernard, J. M. (1979) 'Supervisory training: a discrimination model', *Counsellor Education and Supervision*, (USA), 27, 500–9.

Bion, W. (1961). *Experiences in Groups*. London, Tavistock.

(1974). *Brazilian Lectures 1*. Rio de Janeiro, Imago Editora.

Blake, R., Avis and Mouton, J. (1966). *Corporate Darwinism*. Houston, Texas, Gulf Publishing.

Borders, L. D. and Leddick, G. R. (1987). *Handbook of Counseling Supervision*. Alexandria Virginia, Association for Counsellor Education and Supervision.

Boyd, J. (1978). *Counsellor Supervision: Approaches, Preparation, Practices*. Muncie, Indiana, Accelerated Development.

Brown, A. (1984). *Consultation: an Aid to Effective Social Work*. London, Heinemann.

Butler-Sloss, E. (1988). *Report of the Inquiry in Child Abuse in Cleveland 1987*. London, Her Majesty's Stationery Office. Cm 412.

Campbell, B. (1988). *Unofficial Secrets: Child Sexual Abuse. The Cleveland Case*. London, Virago.

Caplan, G. (1970). *The Theory and Practice of Mental Health Consultation*. London, Tavistock.

Carifio, M. S. and Hess, A. K. (1987). 'Who is the ideal supervisor?' *Professional Psychology: Research and Practice*, (USA), 18, 244–50.

Carroll, M. (1987). Privately circulated paper. Roehampton Institute, University of Surrey.

Casement, P. (1985). *On Learning From the Patient*. London, Tavistock.

Casey, D. (1985). 'When is a team not a team?', *Personnel management*, London, January 26–9.

Cherniss, C. (1980). *Staff Burnout*. Beverly Hills, Sage.

Cherniss, C. and Egnatios, E. (1978). 'Clinical Supervision in Community Mental Health', *Social Work*, London 23/2, 219–23.

Claxton, G. (1984). *Live and Learn*. London, Harper & Row.

Coche, E. (1977). 'Training of group therapists', in Kaslow, F. W. (ed.) *Supervision, Consultation and Staff Training in the Helping Professions*. San Francisco, Josey Bass.

Davies, H. (1987). Interview with Robin Shohet.

Dearnley, B. (1985). 'A plain man's guide to supervision', *Journal of Social Work Practice*, November, 52–65.

De Mello, A. (1985). *One Minute Wisdom*. Anand India, Gujarat Sahitya Prakash.

Doehrman, M. J. G. (1976). 'Parallel processes in supervision and psychotherapy', *Bulletin of the Menninger Clinic*, (USA), 40, part 1.

Edelwich, J. and Brodsky, A. (1980). *Burn-Out*. New York, Human Sciences.

Ekstein, R. (1969). 'Concerning the teaching and learning of psychoanalysis', *Journal of the American Psychoanalytic Association* (USA), 17(2). 312–32.

Ekstein, R. and Wallerstein, R. W. (1972). *The Teaching and Learning of Psychotherapy*. New York, International Universities Press.

Ellis, M. V. and Dell, D. M. (1986). 'Dimensionality of supervisor roles: supervisor perception of supervision', *Journal of Counseling Psychology* (USA), 33 (3), 282–91.

Ernst, S. and Goddison, L. (1981). *In our Own Hands: A Book of Self-Help Therapy*. London, Heinemann.

Fineman, S. (1985). *Social Work Stress and Intervention*. Aldershot, Gower.

Fink, S. C., Beak, J. and Taddeo, K, (1971). 'Organizational crisis and change', *Journal of Applied Behavioural Science* (USA), 17 (1), 14–37.

Frankham, H. (1987). *Aspects of Supervision*, M.Sc. dissertation. Roehampton Institute, University of Surrey.

Freeman, E. (1985). 'The importance of feedback in clinical supervision: implications for direct practice', *The Clinical Supervisor*, 3 (1), 5–26.

Freud, S. (1927). *The Future of Illusion*. Standard Edition 21, London, Hogarth Press.

Friedlander, M. L. and Ward, L. G. (1984). 'Development and validation of the supervisory styles inventory', *Journal of Counseling Psychology*, (USA), 31 (4), 541–57.

Galassi, J. P. and Trent, P. J. (1987). 'A conceptual framework for evaluating supervision effectiveness', *Counselor Education and Supervision* (USA), June, 260–9.

Garratt, B. (1987). *The Learning Organization*. London, Fontana/Collins.

George, M. Hawkins, P. and McLean, A. (1988). *Organizational Culture Manual*. Bath Associates. 6 Vane Street, Bath.

Gittermann, A. and Miller, I. (1977). 'Supervisors as educators', in Kaslow, F. W. (ed.) *Supervision, Consultation and Staff Training in the Helping Professions*. San Francisco, Josey Bass.

Golembiewski, R. T. (1976). *Learning and Change in Groups*. London, Penguin.

Guggenbühl-Craig, A. (1971). *Power in the Helping Professions*. Dallas, Spring.

Hale, K. K. and Stoltenberg, C. D. (forthcoming). 'The effects of self-awareness and evaluation apprehension on counselor trainee anxiety', *The Clinical Supervisor*.

Handy, C. (1976). *Understanding Organizations*. London, Penguin.

Hawkins, P. (1979). 'Staff learning in therapeutic communities', in Hinshelwood, R. and Manning, N. (eds) *Therapeutic Communities, Reflections and Progress*. London, Routledge and Kegan Paul.

(1980). 'Between Scylla and Charybdis', in Jansen, E. (ed.) *The Therapeutic Community Outside of the Hospital.* London, Croom Helm.

(1982). 'Mapping it out', *Community Care,* 22 July, 17–19.

(1985). 'Humanistic psychotherapy supervision: a conceptual framework', *Self and Society: European Journal of Humanistic Psychology,* 13 (2), 69–77.

(1986). 'Living the Learning' Ph.D. thesis, University of Bath.

(1988). 'A Phenomenological psychodrama workshop', in Reason, P. (ed.) *Human Inquiry in Action.* London, Sage.

(1989). 'The social learning approach to day and residential centres', in Brown, A. and Clough, R. (eds) *Groups and Groupings: Life and Work in Day and Residential Settings.* London, Tavistock.

Hawthorne, L. (1975). 'Games supervisors play', *Social Work,* London, 20 May, 179–83.

Herman, N. (1987). *Why Psychotherapy?* London, Free Association Books.

Heron, J. (1974). *Reciprocal Counselling.* Guildford, Surrey, University of Surrey Human Potential Research Project.

(1975). *Six-Category Intervention Analysis.* Guildford, Surrey: University of Surrey. Human Potential Research Project.

Hess, A. K. (ed.) (1980). *Psychotherapy Supervision: Theory, Research and Practice.* New York, Wiley.

(1987). 'Psychotherapy supervision: stages, Buber and a theory of relationship', *Professional Psychology: Research and Practice* (USA), 18 (3), 251–9.

Hickman, C. R. and Silva, M. A. (1985). *Creating Excellence.* London, Allen & Unwin.

Hillman, J. (1979). *Insearch: Psychology and Religion.* Dallas, Texas, Spring.

Hinshelwood, R. and Manning, N. (1979). *Therapeutic Communities: Reflections and Progress.* London, Routledge and Kegan Paul.

Hogan, R. A. (1964). 'Issues and approaches in supervision', *Psychotherapy: Theory, Research and Practice,* 1, 139–41.

Holloway, E. L. (1984). 'Outcome evaluation in supervision research', *The Counseling Psychologist* (USA), 12 (3), 167–74.

(1987). 'Developmental models of supervision: is it development?', *Professional Psychology: Research and Practice* 18 (3), 209–16.

Holloway, E. L. and Johnston, R. (1985). 'Group supervision: widely practiced but poorly understood', *Counselor Education and Supervision* (USA), June, 332–9.

Houston, G. (1985). 'Group supervision of groupwork', *Self and Society: European Journal of Humanistic Psychology,* XIII (2), 64–6.

Hunt, P. (1966). 'Supervision', *Marriage Guidance,* Spring, 15–22.

Illich, I. (1973). *Deschooling Society.* London, Penguin.

Jamplosky, G. (1979). *Love is Letting Go of Fear.* Berkeley, California, Celestial Arts.

Jones, M. (1982). *The Process of Change.* London, Routledge and Kegan Paul.

Jourard, S. (1971). *The Transparent Self.* New York, Van Nostrand.

Juch, B. (1983). *Personal Development.* Chichester, Wiley.

Kadushin, A. (1968). 'Games people play in supervision', *Social Work* (USA), 13.

(1976). *Supervision in Social Work.* New York, Columbia University Press.

(1977). *Consultation in Social Work.* New York, Columbia University Press.

Kagan, N. (1980). 'Influencing human interaction – eighteen years with IPR)', in Hess, A. K. (ed.) *Psychotherapy Supervision: Theory, Research and Practice.* New York, Wiley.

Kaslow, F. W. (ed.) (1977). *Supervision, Consultation and Staff Training in the Helping Professions.* San Francisco, Josey Bass.

Kelly, G. A. (1955). *The Psychology of Personal Constructs,* vols. 1 and 2, New York, Norton.

Kevlin, F. (1987). Interview with Robin Shohet.

(1988). *'Peervision'*. M.Sc. Dissertation, Roehampton Institute, University of Surrey.

Kolb, D. A., Rubin, I. M. and McIntyre, J. M. (1971). *Organizational Psychology: an Experiential Approach*. New York, Prentice Hall.

Lambert, M. J. and Arnold, R. C. (1987). 'Research and the supervisory process', *Professional Psychology: Research and Practice*, (USA), 18 (3), 217–24.

Langs, R. (1978). *The Listening Process*. New York, Jason Aronson.

(1983). *The Supervisory Experience*. New York, Jason Aronson.

(1985). *Workbook for Psychotherapists*. Emerson, New Jersey, Newconcept Press.

Lewin, K. (1952). 'Defining the field at a given time', in Cartwright, D. (ed.) *Field Theory in Social Sciences*. London, Tavistock.

Liddle, B. J. (1986). 'Resistance to supervision: a response to perceived threat', *Counselor Education and Supervision*, (USA), December, 117–27.

Lievegoed, B. C. J. (1973). *The Developing Organisation*. London, Tavistock.

Liss, J. (1985). 'Using mime and re-enactment to supervise body orientated therapy', *Self and Society: European Journal of Humanistic Psychology*, XIII (2), 82–5.

Loganbill, C., Hardy, E. and Delworth, U. (1982). 'Supervision, a conceptual model', *The Counseling Psychologist*, USA, 10(1), 3–42.

McBride, M. C. and Martin, G. E. (1986). 'Dual-focus supervision: a non-apprenticeship approach', *Counselor Education and Supervision* (USA), March, 175–82.

McLean, A. (1986). 'Accessing Organization Cultures'. Working paper, University of Bath.

McLean, A. and Marshall, J. (1988). *Working with Cultures: A Workbook for People in Local Government*. Luton, Local Government Training Board.

Marken, M. and Payne, M. (undated) *Enabling and Ensuring*. Leicester National Youth Bureau and Council for Education and Training in Youth and Community Work.

Marshall, J. (1982). 'Job Stressors: Recent Research in a Variety of Occupations'. Paper presented to the 20th International Congress of Applied Psychology, Edinburgh.

Martin, J. S., Goodyear, R. K. and Newton, F. B. (1987). 'Clinical supervision: an intensive case study', *Professional Psychology: Research and Practice* (USA), 18 (3), 225–35.

Maslach, C. (1982). 'Understanding burnout: definitional issues in analysing a complex phenomenon', in Poine, W. S. (ed.) *Job Stress and Burnout*. Beverley Hills, Sage.

Mattinson, J. (1975). *The Reflection Process in Casework Supervision*. London, Institute of Marital Studies.

Menzies, I. (1970). *The Functioning of Social Systems as a Defence Against Anxiety*. London, Tavistock Institute of Human Relations.

Munson, C. E. (1987). 'Sex roles and power relationships in supervision', *Professional Psychology: Research and Practice* (USA), 18 (3), 236–43.

O'Toole, L. (1987). *'Counselling skills and self-awareness training: their effect on mental well being and job satisfaction in student nurses'*, M.Sc. Dissertation, Roehampton Institute, University of Surrey.

Payne, C. and Scott, T. (1982). *Developing Supervision of Teams in Field and Residential Social Work*. London, National Institute of Social Work, Paper no. 12.

Peters, T. J. and Waterman, R. H. (1982). *In Search of Excellence*. New York, Harper and Row.

Pines, A. M. Aronson, E. and Kafry, D. (1981). *Burnout: From Tedium to Growth*.

New York, The Free Press.

Plant, R. (1987), *Managing Change and Making it Stick*. London, Fontana/Collins.

Ponterotto, J. G. and Zander, T. A. (1984). 'A multimodal approach to counsellor supervision', *Counsellor Education and Supervision* (USA), 24, 40–50.

Proctor, B. (undated) 'Supervision: A co-operative exercise in accountability'; Marken, M. and Payne, M. (eds), *Enabling and Ensuring*. Leicester National Youth Bureau and Council for Education and Training in Youth and Community Work.

  (1988). *Supervision a Working Alliance*. (videotape training manual). St Leonards-on-sea, East Sussex, Alexia Publications.

Ram Dass and Gorman, P. (1985). *How can I help*. London, Rider.

Revans, R. W. (1982). *The Origins and Growth of Action Learning*. London, Chartwell-Bratt, Bromley and Lund.

Rioch, M. J., Coulter, W. R., and Weinberger, D. M. (1976). *Dialogues for Therapists*. San Francisco, Josey Bass.

Rogers, C. R. (1957). 'The necessary and sufficient conditions of therapeutic personality change', *Journal of Counseling Psychology* (USA), 21, 95–103.

Rowan, J. (1983). *Reality Game: A Guide to Humanistic Counselling and Therapy*. London, Routledge and Kegan Paul.

Sansbury, D. L. (1982). 'Developmental supervision from a skills perspective', *The Counseling psychologist* (USA), 10(1), 53–7.

Savickas, M. L., Marquart, C. D. and Supinski, C. R. (1986). 'Effective supervision in groups', *The Counseling Psychologist* (USA), September, 17–25.

Schutz, W. C. (1973). *Elements of Encounter*. Big Sur, California, Joy Press.

Searles, H. F. (1955). 'The informational value of the supervisor's emotional experience', *Collected Papers on Schizophrenia and Related Subjects*. London, Hogarth Press.

  (1975). 'The patient as therapist to the analyst', in Langs, R. (ed.) *Classics in Psychoanalytic Technique*. New York, Jason Aronson.

Shainberg, D. (1983). 'Teaching therapists to be with their clients', in Westwood, J. (ed.), *Awakening the Heart*. Colorado, Shambhala.

Shearer, A. (1983). Who saves the social workers? London, *Guardian*, 6 July.

Shohet, R. (1985). *Dreamsharing*. Northamptonshire, Turnstone Press.

Shohet, R., Hawkins, P. and Wilmot, J. (forthcoming). *Supervision Workbook*.

Smith, D. (1985). 'The client as supervisor: the approach of Robert Langs', *Self and Society: European Journal of Humanistic Psychology*, XIII (2), 92–5.

Spice, C. G. Jr. and Spice, W. H. (1976). 'A triadic method of supervision in the training of counselors and counseling supervisors', *Counselor Education and Supervision* (USA), 15, 251–8.

Stoltenberg, C. D. and Delworth, U. (1987). *Supervising Counselors and Therapists*. San Francisco, Josey Bass.

Symington, N. (1986). *The Analytic Experience*. London, Free Association Books.

Tonnesmann, M. (1979). 'The Human Encounter in the Helping Professions', London Fourth Winnicott Conference, London, March.

Tuckman, B. W. (1965). 'Developmental sequences in small groups', *Psychological Bulletin*, 63 (6), 384–99.

Wilmot, J. and Shohet, R. (1985). 'Paralleling in the supervision process', *Self and Society: European Journal of Humanistic Psychology*, XIII (2), 86–92.

Winnicott, D. W. (1965). *Maturational Processes and the Facilitating Environment*. London, Hogarth Press.

Winnicott, D. W. (1971). *Playing and Reality*. London, Tavistock.

Worthington, E. L. (1987). 'Changes in supervision as counselors and supervisors gain experience: a review', *Professional Psychology: Research and Practice*, 18 (3), 189–208.

Resources

National organizations for counselling and psychotherapy

British Association of Counselling, 37a Sheep Street, Rugby, Warwickshire, CV21 3BX.
United Kingdom Standing Conference for Psychotherapy, Hon Sec: Dorothy Hamilton, 167 Sumatra Road, West Hampstead, London NW6 1PN.

Organizations that offer training in supervision of counsellors and psychotherapists

Centre for Staff Team Development, 31 Lancaster Road, London W11 1QJ and 285 Bloomfield Road, Bath BA2 2NU.
Metanoia, 13 North Common Road, Ealing, London W5 2QB.
Brigid Proctor and Francesca Inskip, 4 Ducks Walk, Twickenham, Middlesex.
Roehampton Institute, Department of Psychology, Digby Stuart College, Roehampton Vale, Roehampton, London SW15 5PU.
Spectrum, 7 Endymion Road, Finsbury Park, London N4 1EE.
The Tavistock Clinic, 120 Belsize Lane, London NW3 5BA.
The Westminster Pastoral Foundation, 23 Kensington Square, London. W8 5HN.

For training in supervision for the other helping professions, contact the appropriate professional organization

British Association of Occupational Therapists, 20 Rede Place, Bayswater, London W2 4TU.
British Association of Social Workers, 16 Kent Street, Birmingham B5 6RD.
British Psychological Society, St Andrews House, 48 Princess Road East, Leicester LE1 7DR.
Central Council for Education and Training in Social Work, Derbyshire House, Chad's Street, London WC1 8AD.
College of Speech Therapists, 6 Lechmere Road, London NW2 5BU.
Council for Education and Training in Youth and Community Work (CETYCW), 17–23 Albion Street, Leicester LE1 6GD.
National Association of Probation Officers, 3/4 Chivalry Road, Battersea, London SW11 1HT.

Royal College of Nursing, 20 Cavendish Square, London W1M 0AB.
Royal College of Psychiatrists, 17 Belgrave Square, London SW1X 8PG.

Training tapes on supervision

Audiotapes
Two audiotapes by Francesca Inskipp and Brigid Proctor:
  'Skills For Supervisees'
  'Skills For Supervisors'
Both £6 each including introductory leaflet.
Videotapes
'Supervision: A Working Alliance', Brigid Proctor and David Willow. £50 for two-
  hour tape and training manual.
All tapes are available from Alexia Publications c/o Brigid Proctor, 4 Ducks Walk,
  Twickenham, Middlesex.

Author Index

Subject Index